THEIR FOOTSTEPS

a collection of travel poems and photographs

KASSIE J RUNYAN

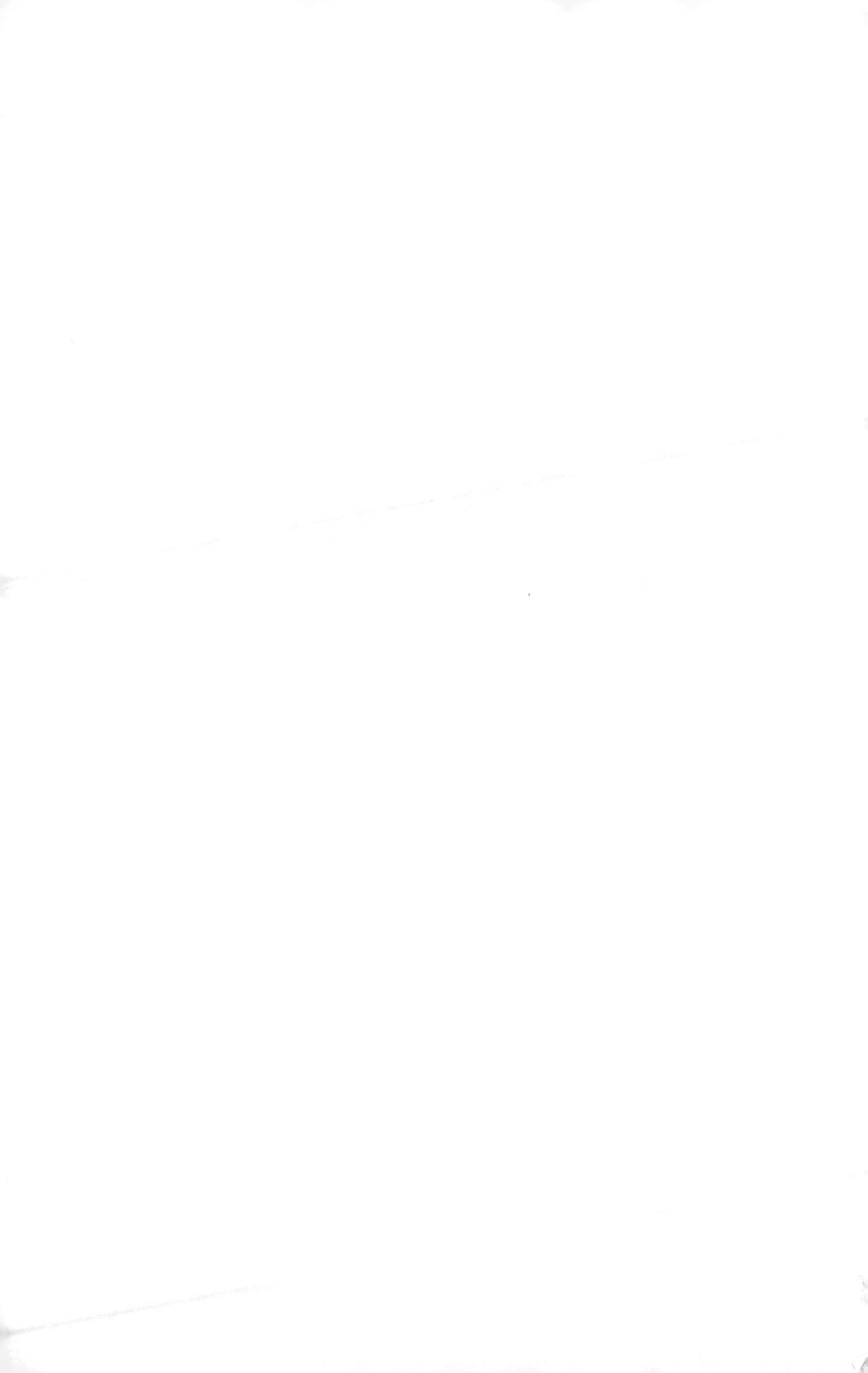

ISBN: 978-1-7355140-2-4

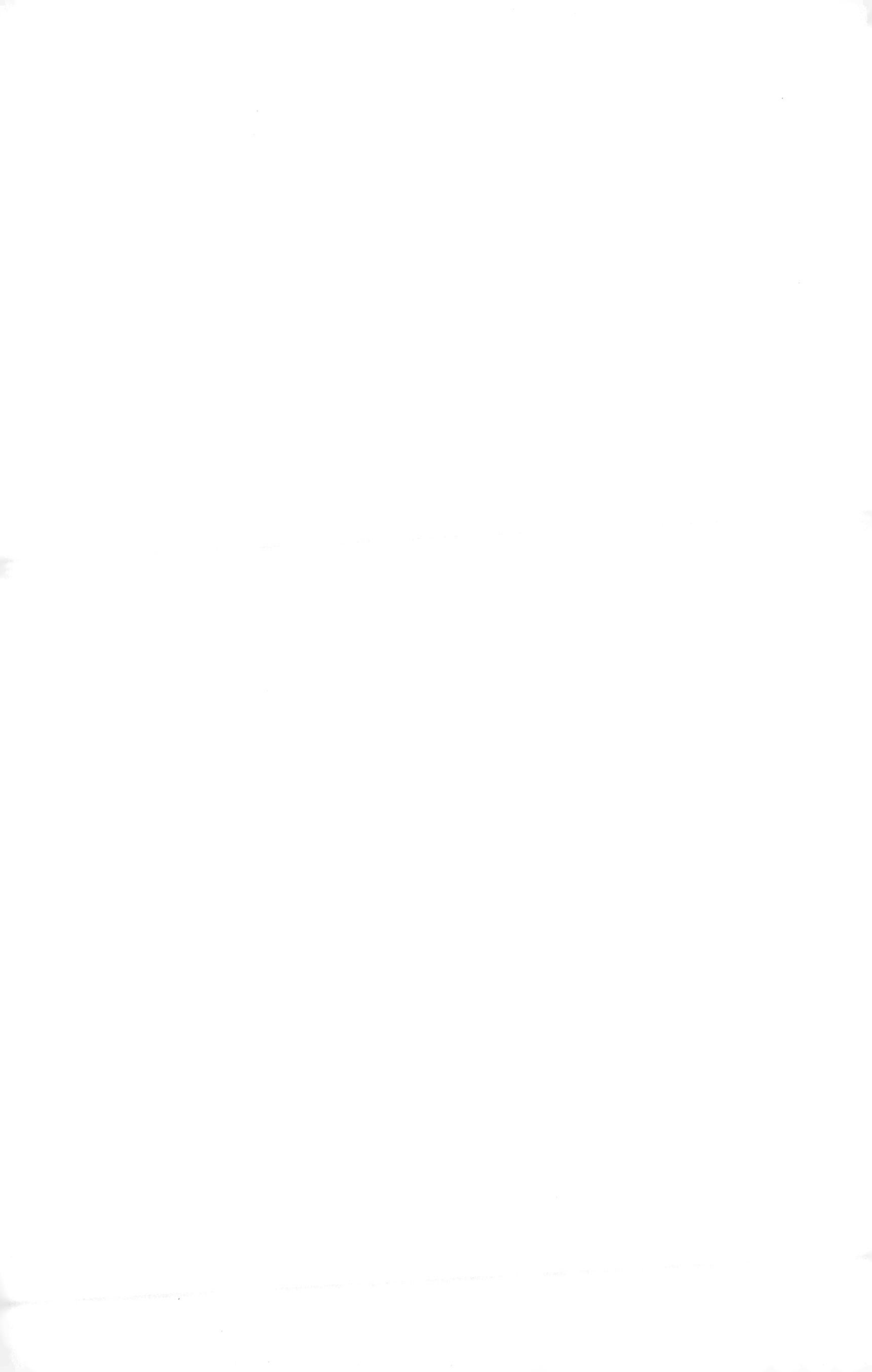

DEDICATION

Dedicated to my husband, otherwise known to me as "The Dude." He is my understanding partner who joins me on boats in rough weather despite his seasickness, is the first to say "Sure, why not?" in response to me saying "We should totally climb that random mountain next to the highway," stands by me as I continue to search for the very edge of our adventure comfort zone, and lets me doodle or write in a notebook for an hour... long after our beer is gone and even though we still have a three-hour drive ahead of us. My travel buddy. My lifetime companion.

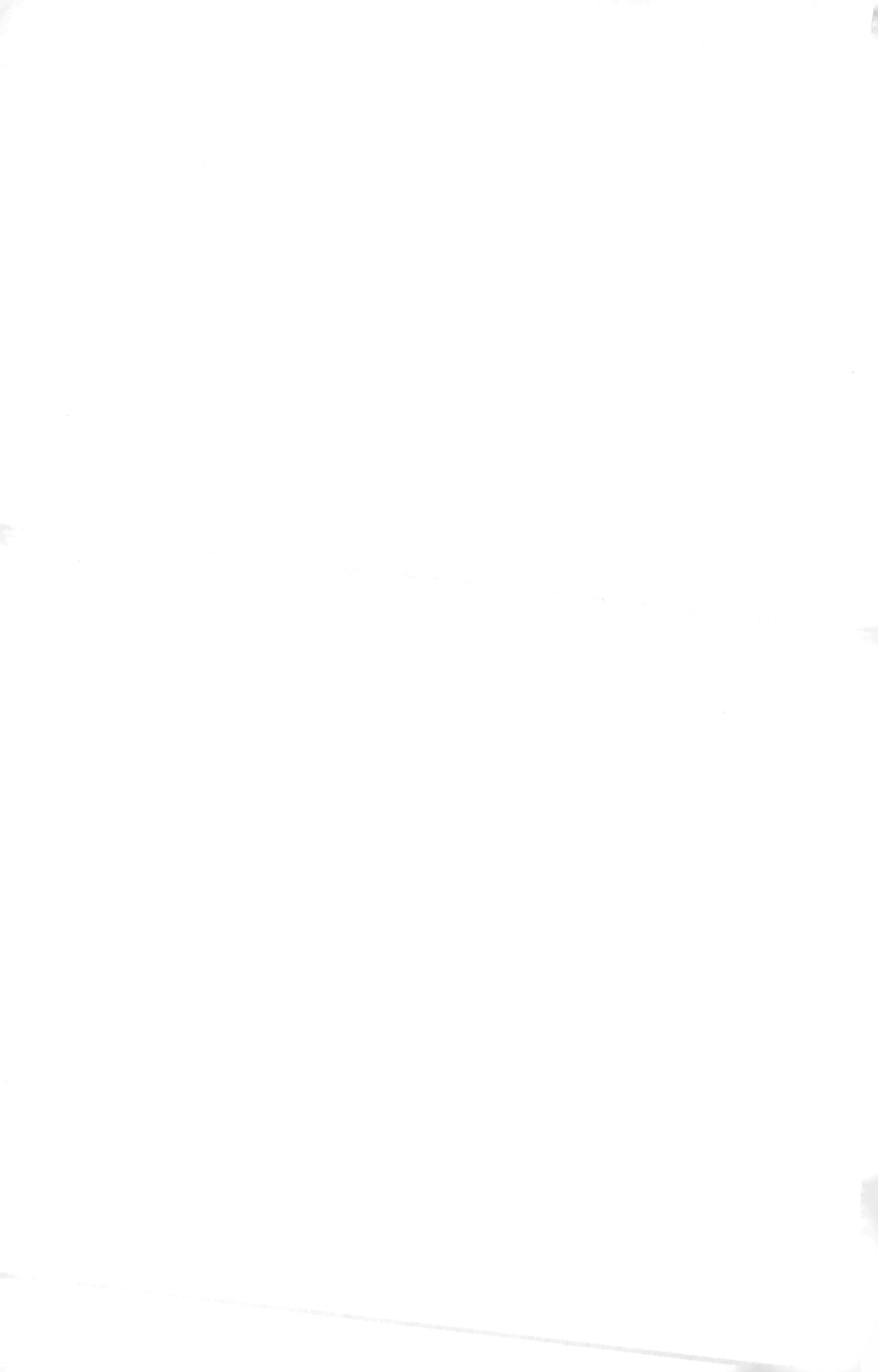

ACKNOWLEDGMENTS

Thank you to my parents. They sparked my passion for exploration as a child (in the written word and physical activity) and made our summer vacation something that I looked forward to every year. As an adult I still look forward to every single moment we get to explore some place new together.

Thank you to my in-laws. They not only raised "The Dude" (a trying task to be sure) but also instilled a love of road trips and Oregon in him – a love that also passed to me when they welcomed me into their family and into their road trips west.

IRISH SEA – PISSED

Back and forth.
Side to side.
The water thrusts and screams.
It's fighting against itself.
Angry.
Pissed.
There in the middle of the clashing waves
is a boat.
A tiny speck full of tiny people.
The captain – determined.
A girl squeezes her eyes tight
as the tiny vessel is tossed by the sea
like it's a toy boat in the bath
of a small child.
The water slams the side.
The rusted bolts strain to hold.
The angry sea breathes in,
quickly.
Out again
sending icy water toward the girl;
her muscles clenched and she sat proud,
trying to convince herself that she wasn't afraid
as the boat pitched and fell towards the deep grey.
The girl could feel the fear building
as the sea tried to swallow her whole
and the ocean ***breathed in.***

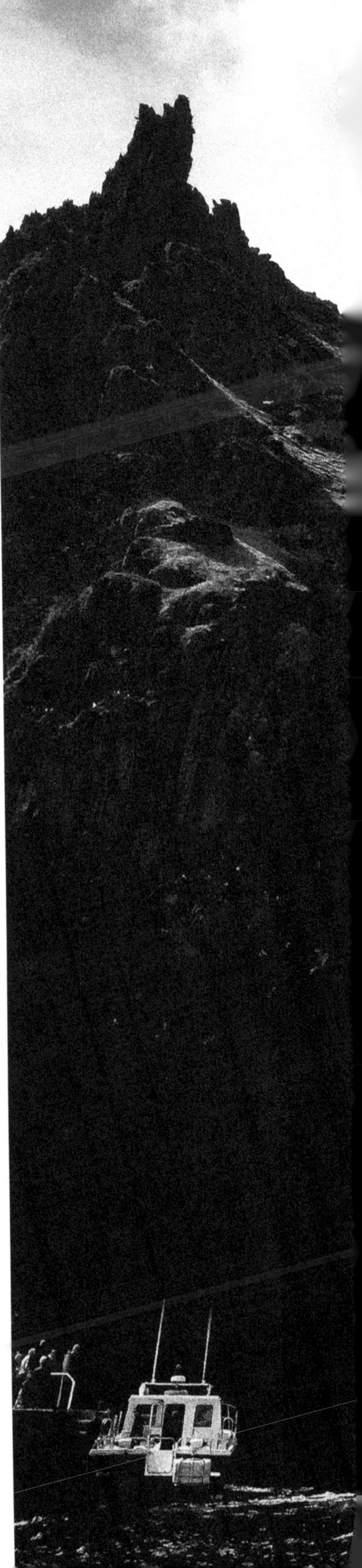

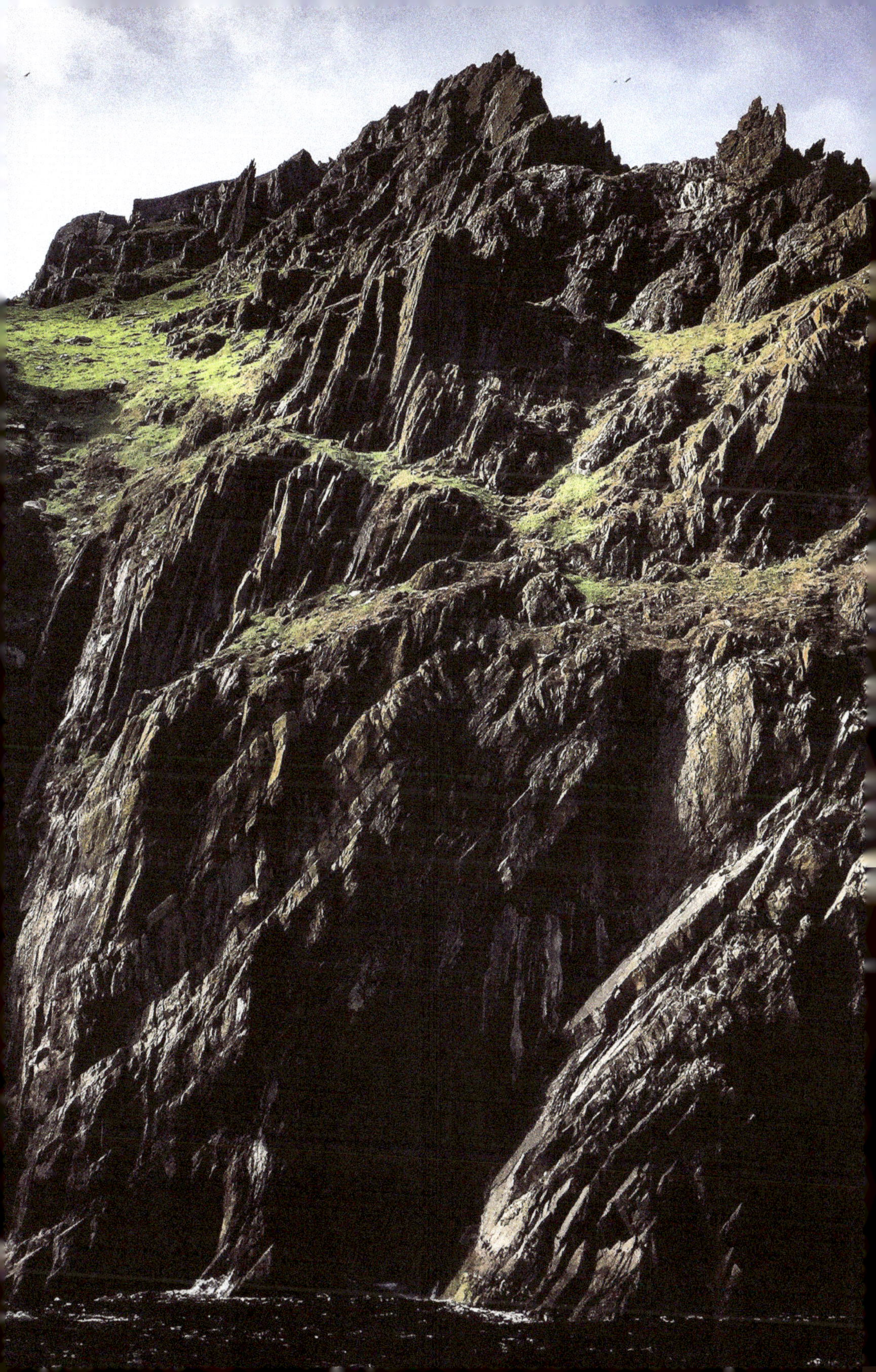

North Atlantic Ocean - Ireland

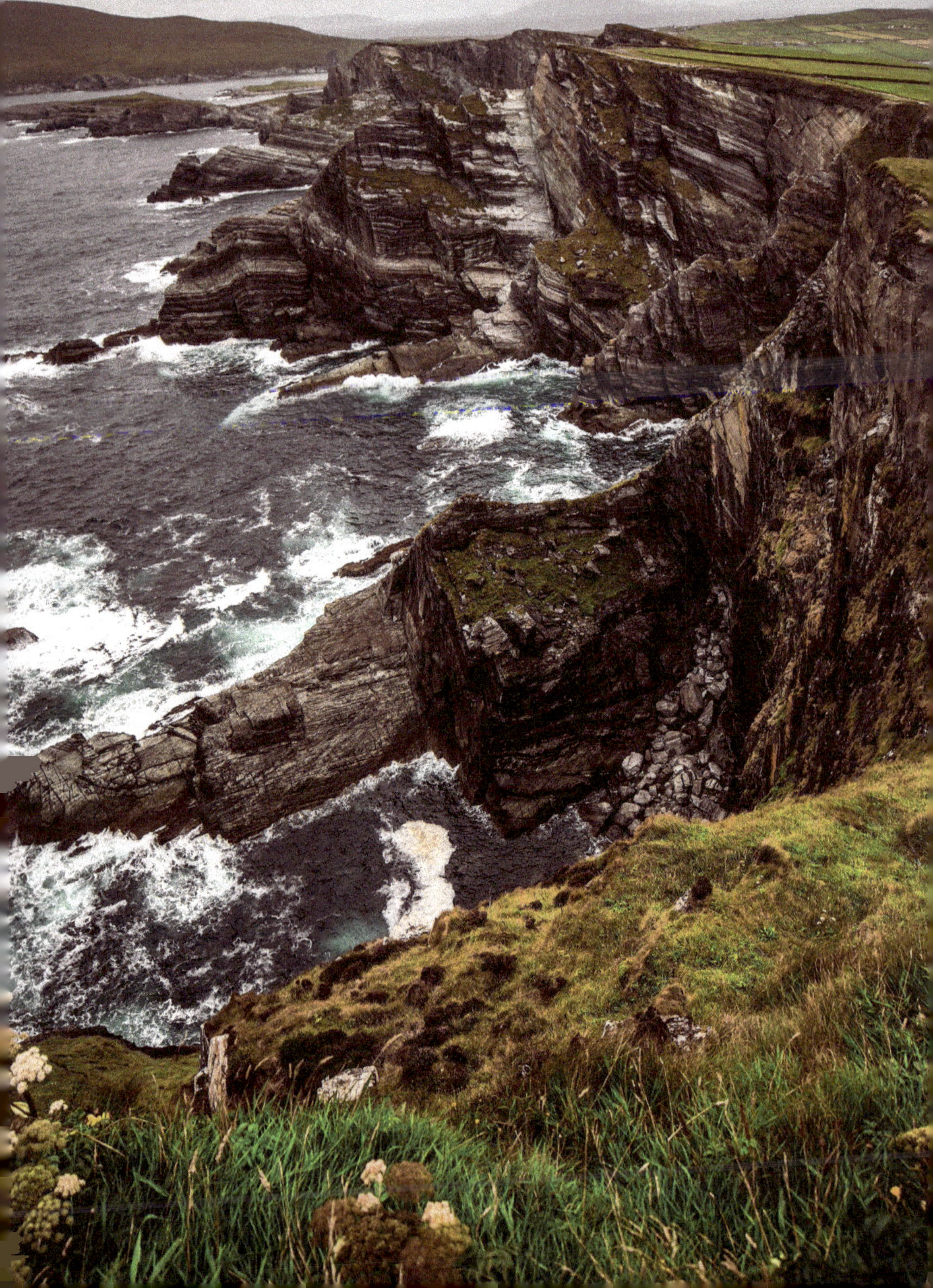

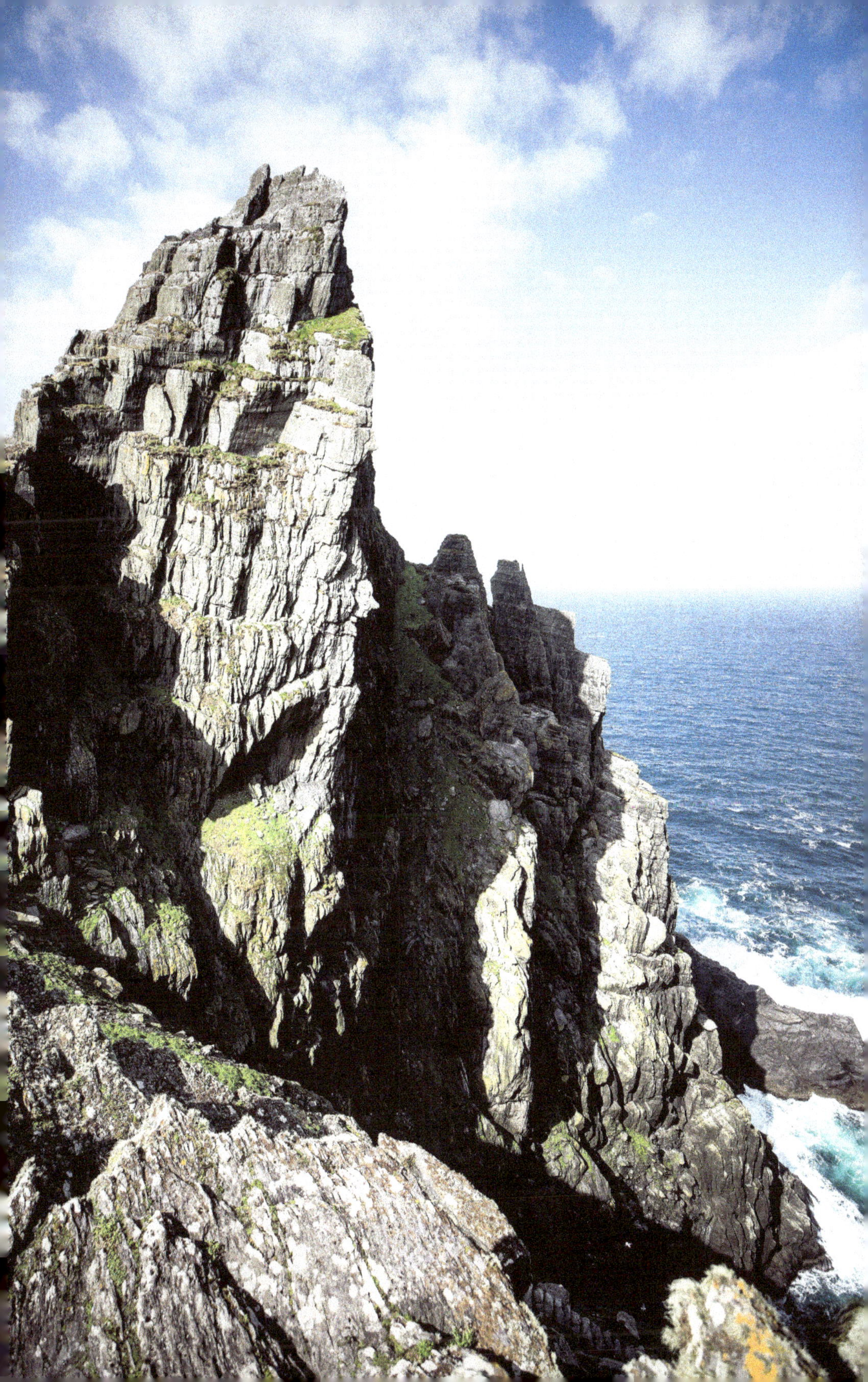

THE DAILY CATCH

My eyes shoot open
to the sound of a horn
coming from the boat
carrying the fisherman home.

I get out of bed
and open the door,
stepping into the night
as the rain drizzles down.
I taste it on my lips,
mixing with the salty smell
of the daily catch.

The water laps against
the side of the bay walls
as the light from the boat
sweeps across the buildings.
A flash of a faded mermaid
painted on the side
of a worn-out building,
telling us what lies beneath.

I breathe in deeply,
one last inhale
of rain and ocean as one,
before turning back to bed,
sinking down
down
down
into the warmth.

The distant but familiar bark
of a sea lion
is quickly joined by others.
The staccato lulls me to sleep
in this cool Oregon night.

My eyes close again
in the place I want to be.

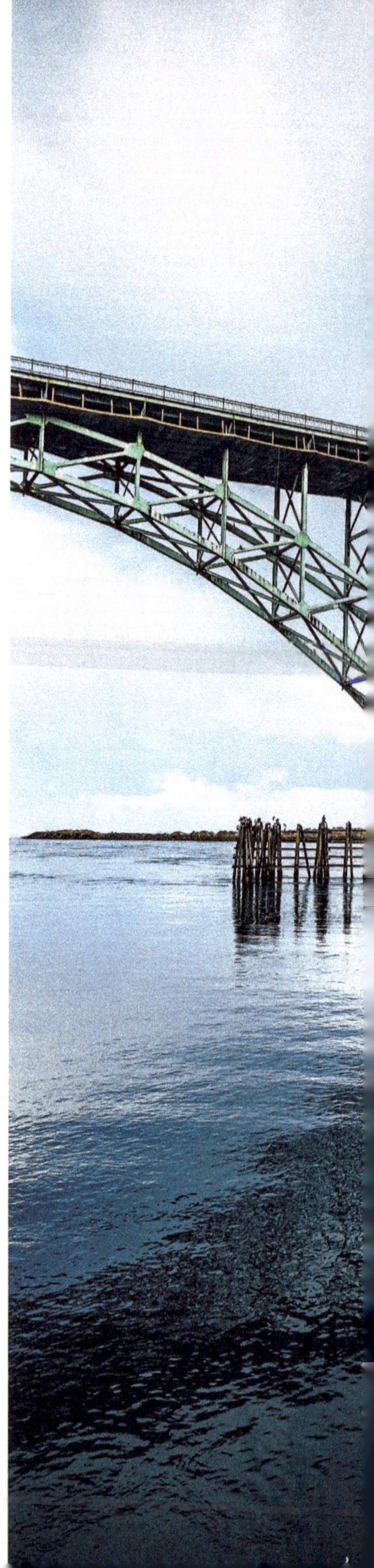

Newport, Oregon, USA

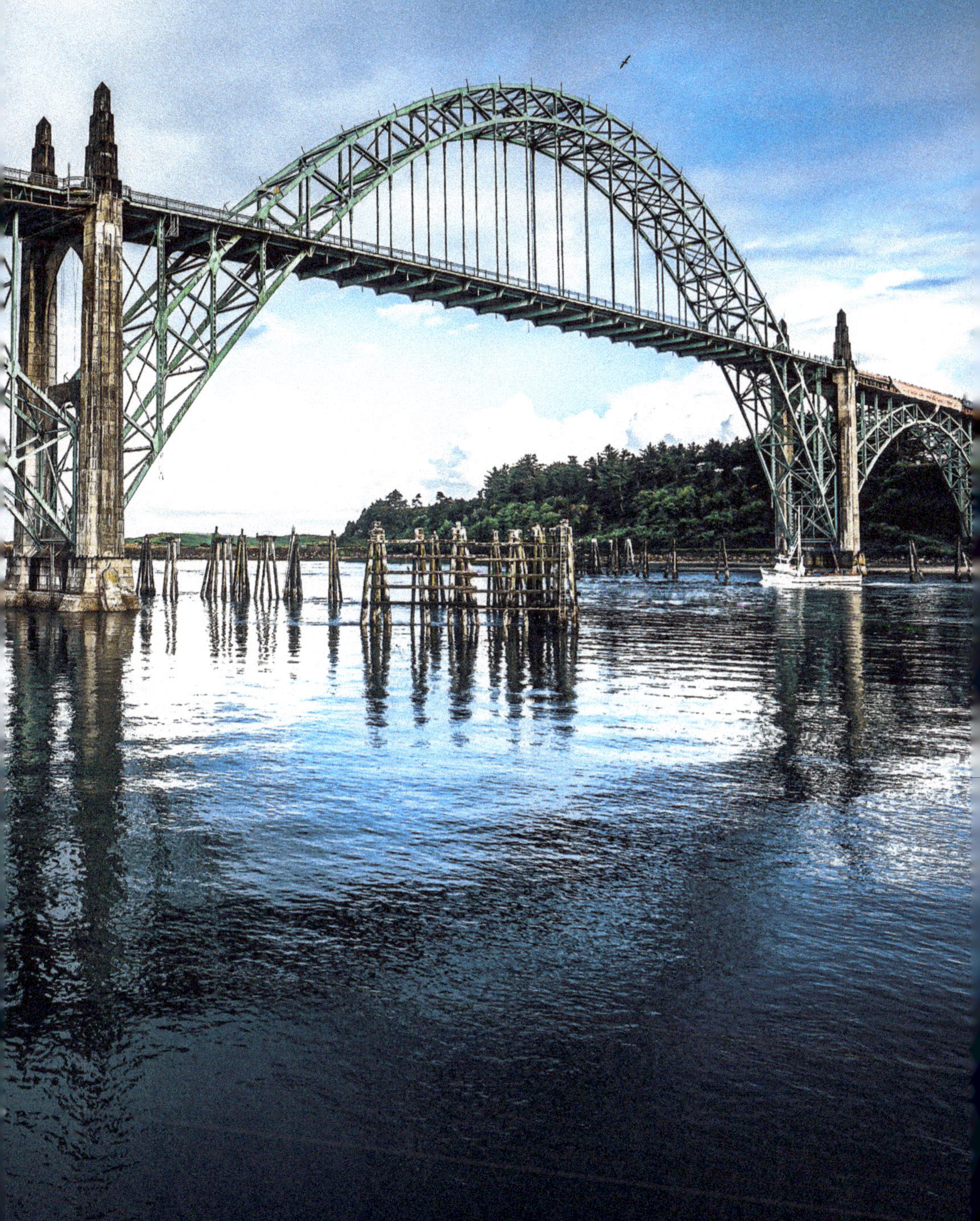

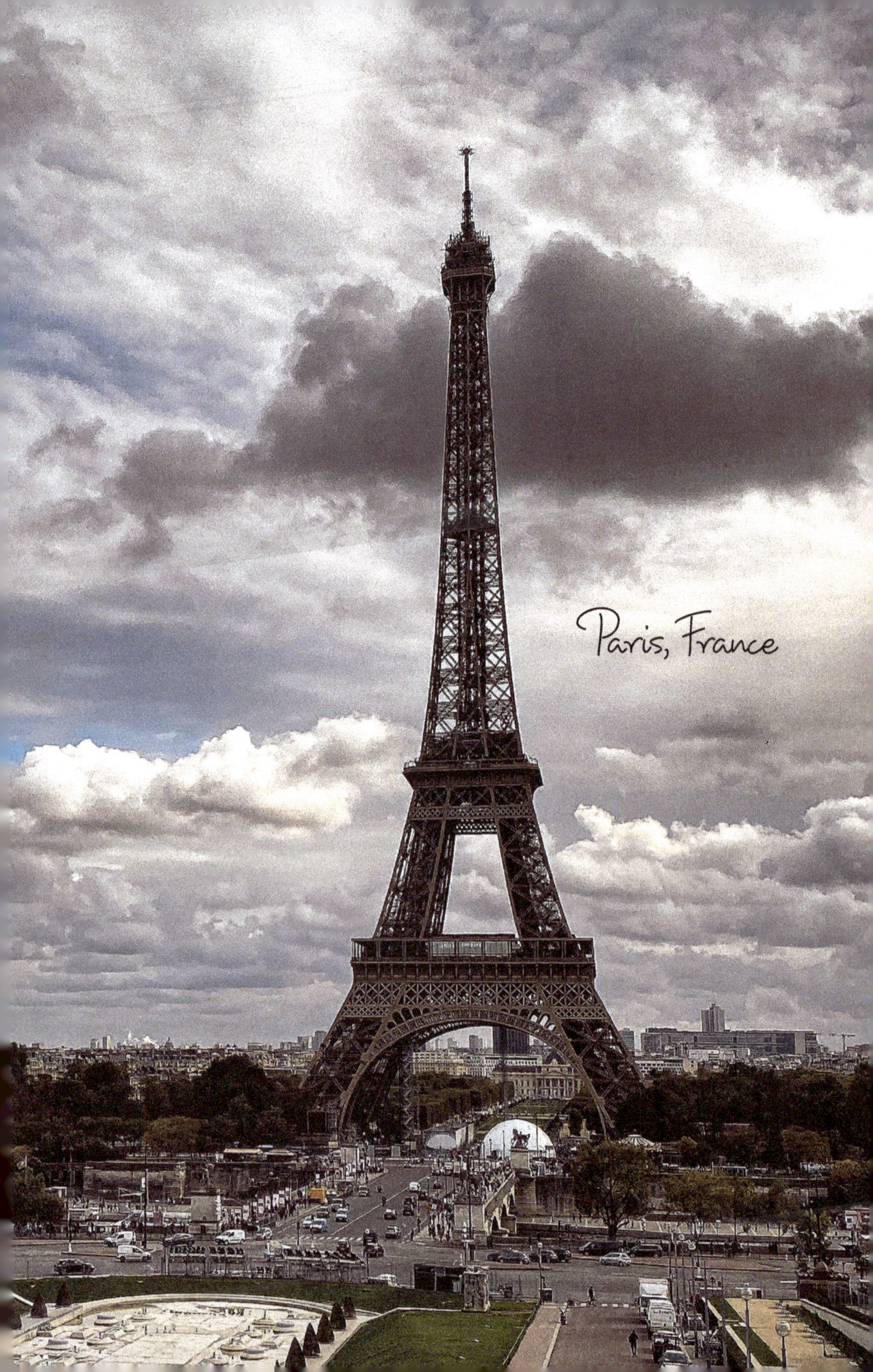
Paris, France

WATER AND LIGHT

The rain pats the covering above.
The smell of cigarettes surrounds me,
hand-rolled of course.
It is mixed with the smell of coffee.
Steam rising from the cups
that are placed between the wine glasses.
I sit at the table sipping on both.
Watching the lights reflect off the wet
cobblestone paths around the café,
I listen to talk of love and art,
all with a French tongue.
The coffee cup warms my cold hands.
Everything dampened from the rain.
A violin plays in the distance,
a song of France's past.
But there is a whisper even older.
A story is shared from every street corner
and down every alley.
The original people called her
"The Place Where Water Shines."
She has been broken and burnt,
and pasted back together
with passion.
If I squint my eyes
I can see the twinkle of stars through the rain
lighting up a tower made of steel
in the center of a city once
old and beat,
now pulled from the rubble
and transformed into
"The City of Light."

TEETH

Back and forth
The boat sways
Out in a bright blue
The waves high
The land far away
My wetsuit is tight
My mind fuzzy
A bird yells
A bird dives
The man points
To the cage
I pull on my mask
And climb down
The waters frozen
I can feel through
The wetsuit
Back and forth
The boat sways
The sun beats down
There is a splash
Someone yells
I remember
And take a deep breath
Then push myself under
The cold cold water

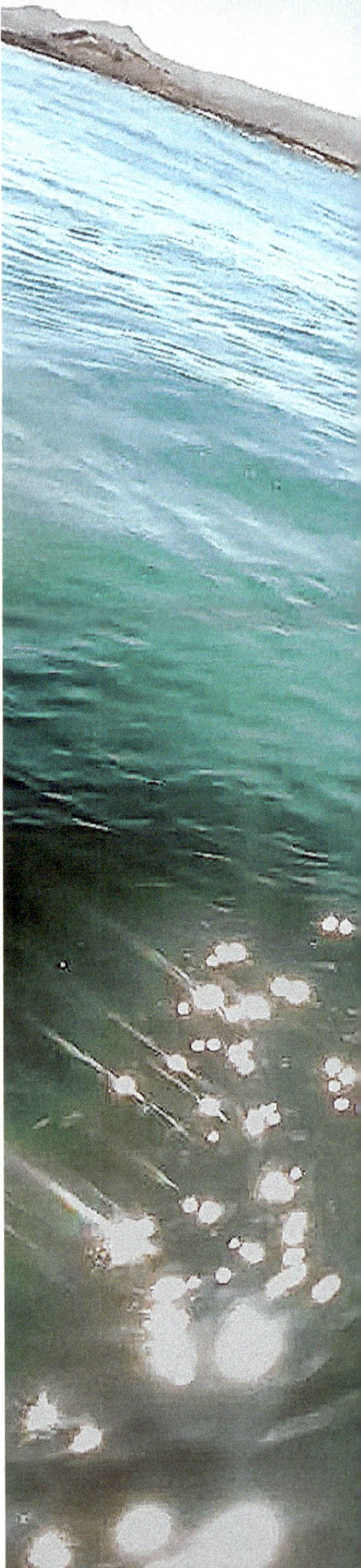

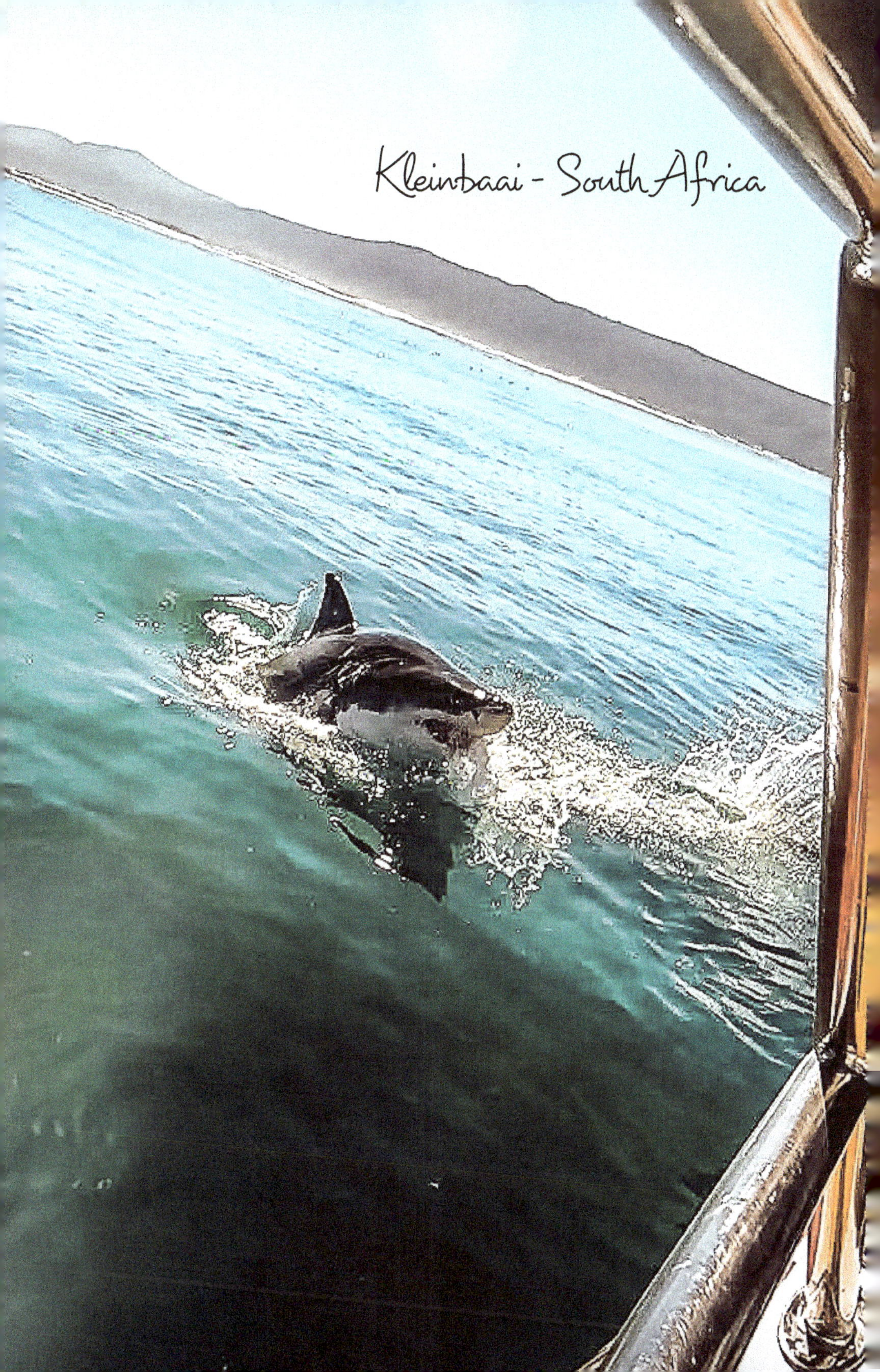
Kleinbaai - South Africa

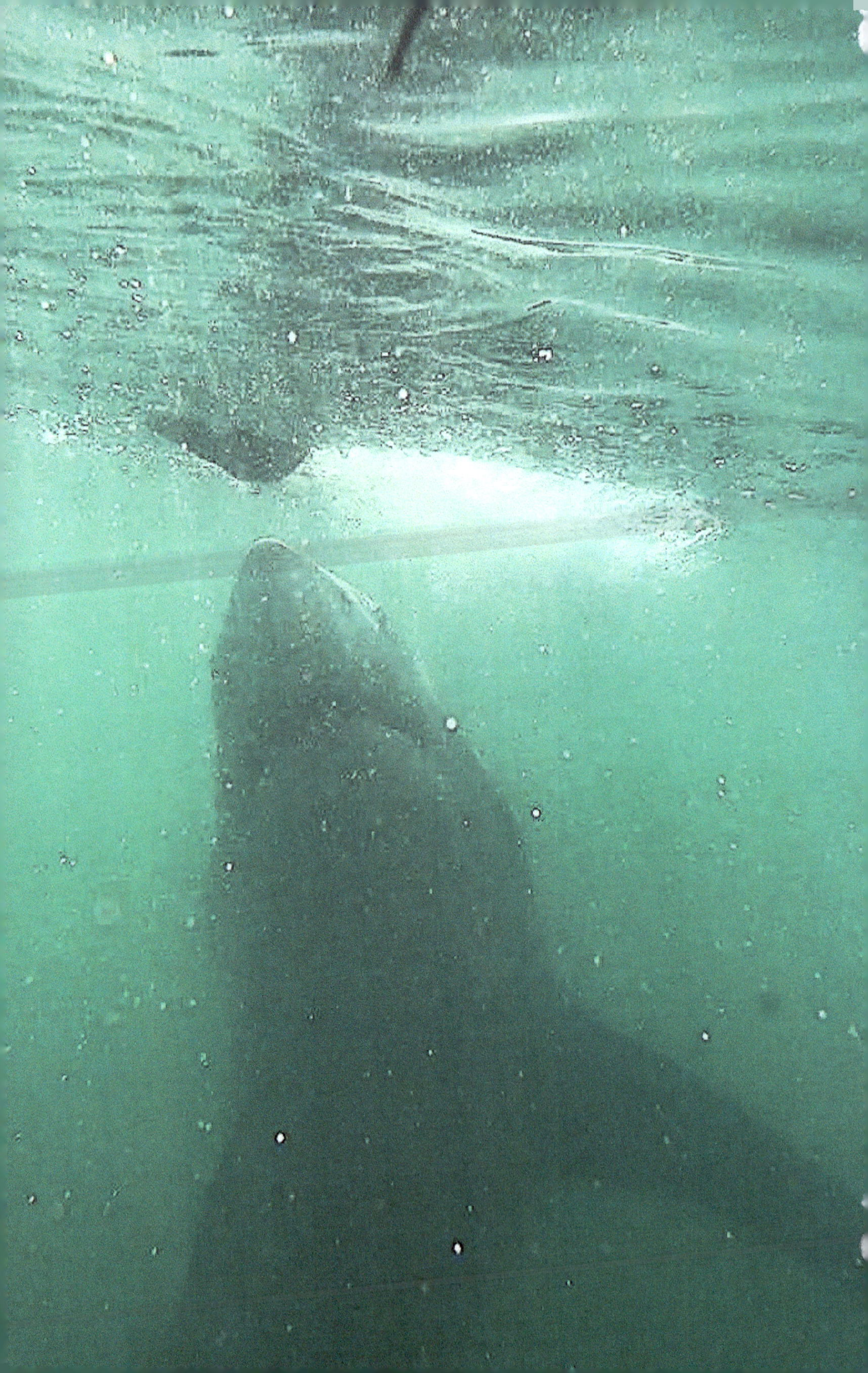

As teeth close
In front of me
SMASH
A tail hits the cage
I lose my air
Leaving me in bubbles
Swim up for more
And back down
Forgetting the cold
A fin
A nose
A beady black eye
Rows of teeth
Open
And close
On the chum
That lays at the top
Of the water
I'm in
Up for a breath
As a shark swims by
Flying out of the water
And down
Splash
A beast
Twice
Three times
My size
As he plays in the water
Looking for a treat

THE NEXT STOP IS...

Heads move
at the same speed.
The woman speaks;
"The next stop is..."
"Sponsored by..."
The car stops.
The heads swerve.
I look around me.
Pink hair in a mohawk.
Rainbow shirts.
The car starts.
The heads move in unison,
all looking down
at their pocket computers.
I look down
at their Vans sneakers.
'90s music blaring
through headphones.
Roses fly past the windows.
Water shines as we fly
over the river...
one of them.
Everyone alone.
Lost in their thoughts
and their music.
As their heads move together
with the speed of the streetcar.
A child laughs.
Everyone smiles,
almost as free as
when we were kids too.
For a moment it feels
like I'm back in the '90s,
happy and a little bit grunge.
My head bobs to the beat.
"The next stop is..."

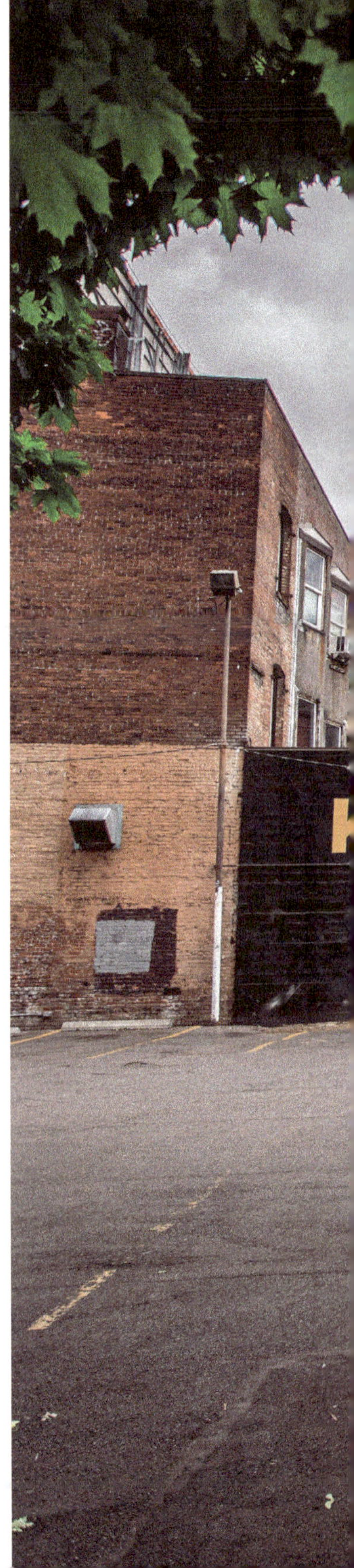

Portland, Oregon, USA

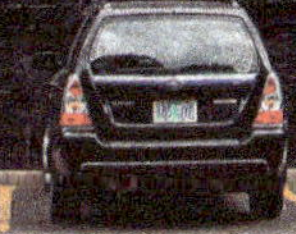

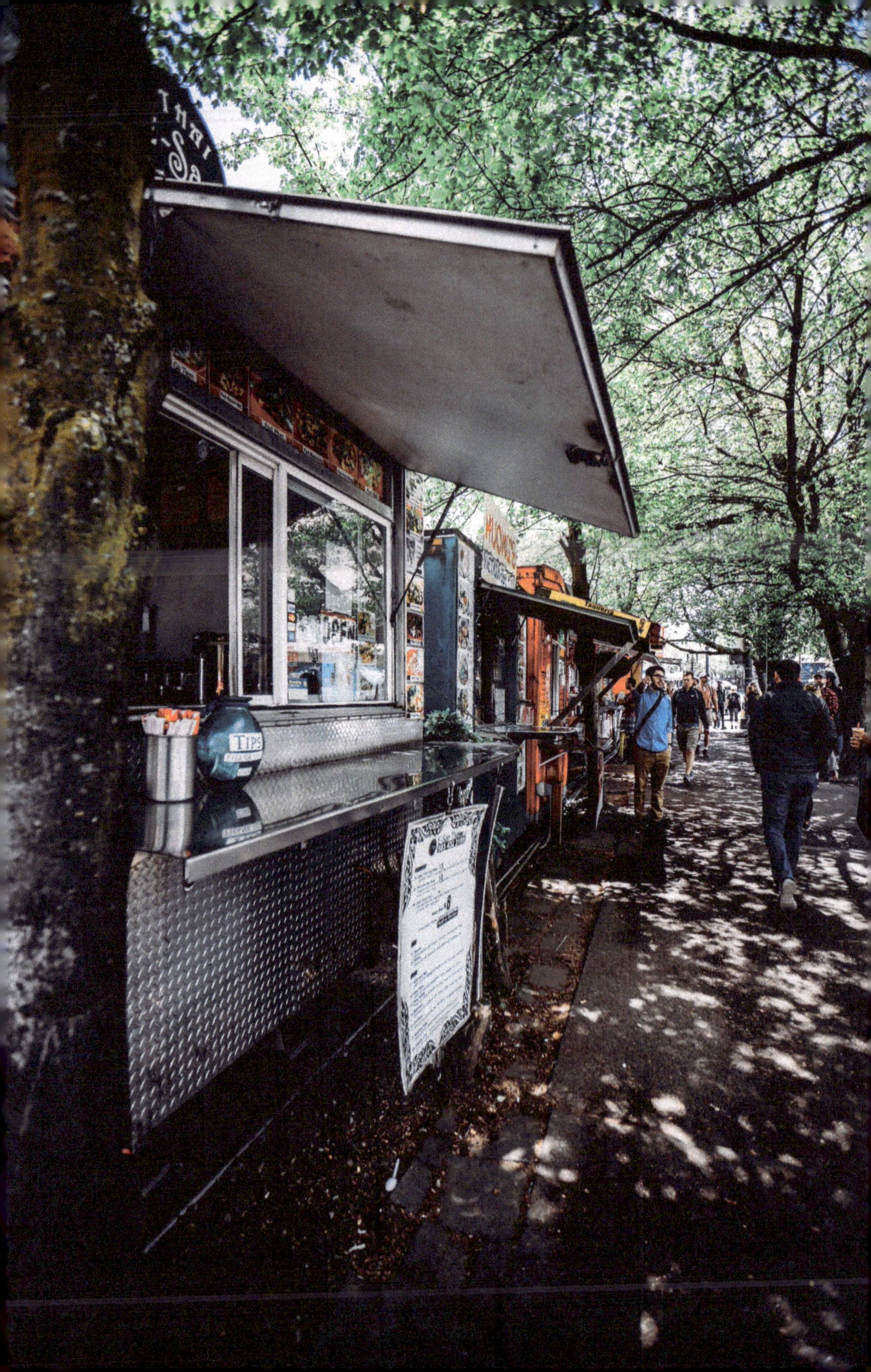
TIPS
OPEN

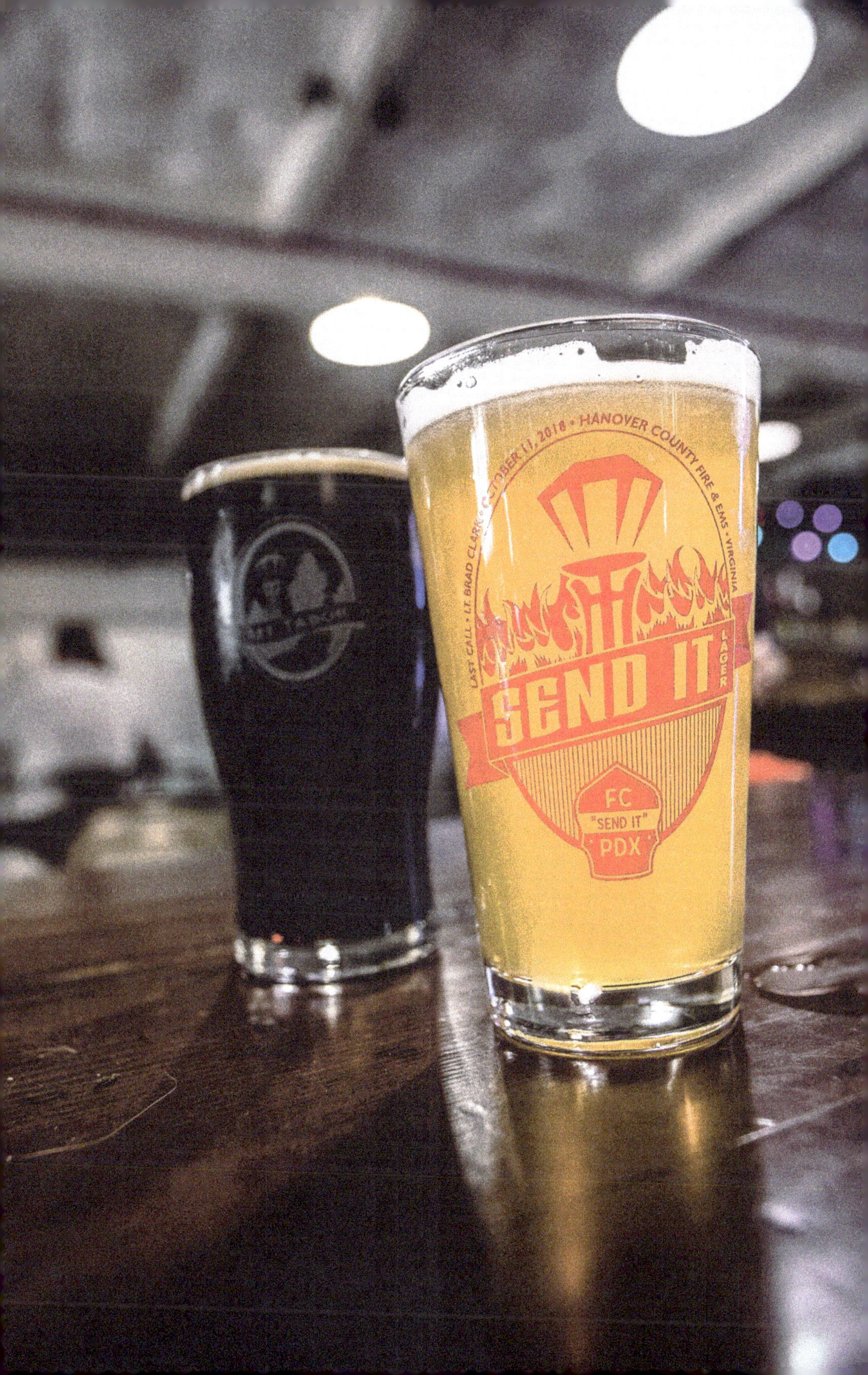
LAST CALL • LT. BRAD CLARK • OCTOBER 11, 2018 • HANOVER COUNTY FIRE & EMS • VIRGINIA
SEND IT
LAGER
FC
"SEND IT"
PDX

TEARS OF STONE

Her face

frozen in time

and stone

Her tears

pausing in their tracks

down her face

for all eternity

Slender body

thrown carelessly

over his grave

by the man who carved her

She will mourn

Forever

Visited by others

still living

Wanting to know

her story

of loss

and pain

that caused her tears

etched in stone

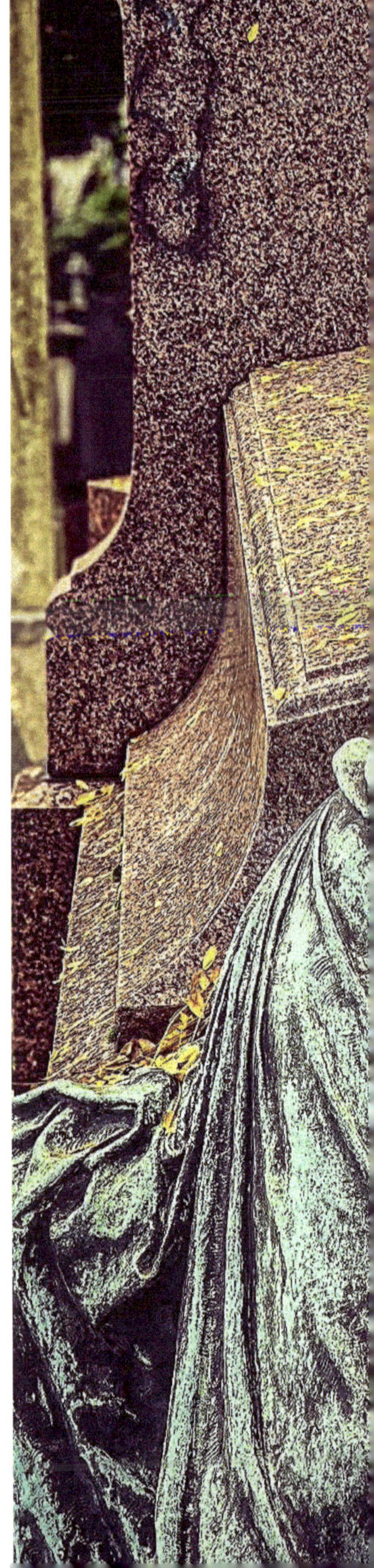

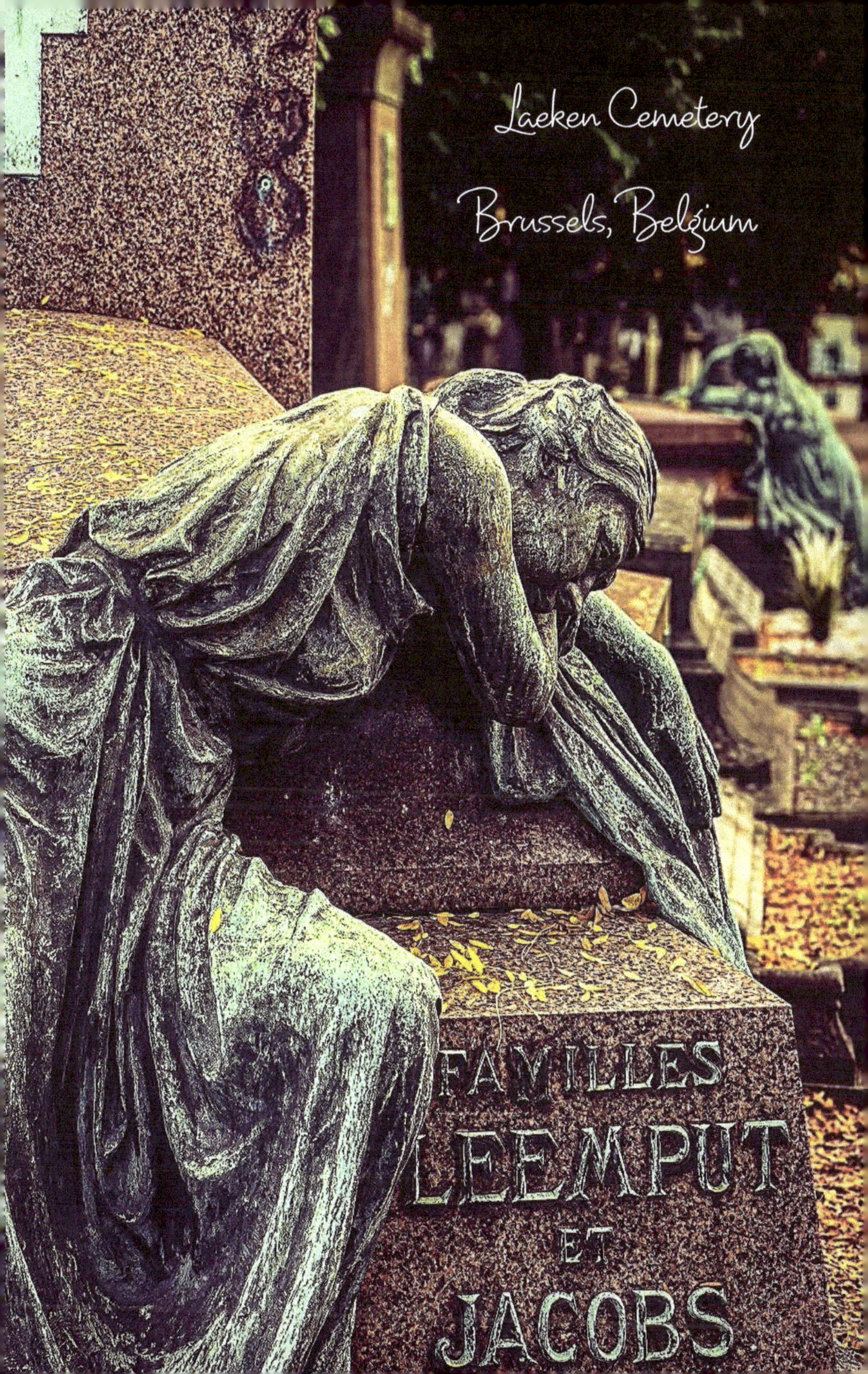

Laeken Cemetery

Brussels, Belgium

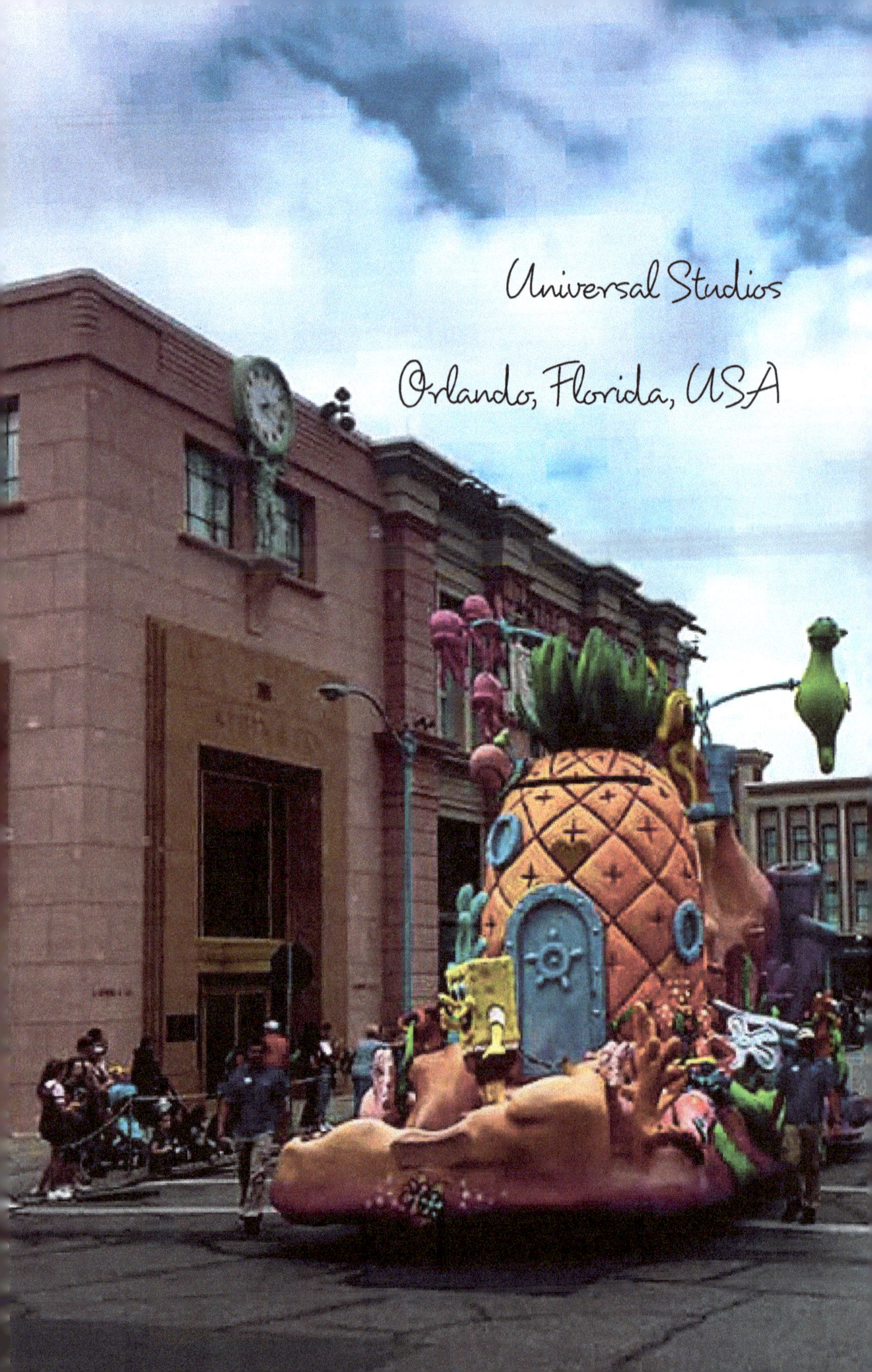
Universal Studios
Orlando, Florida, USA

THE NEON LIGHTS

The air is sweet.
The drinks are sweeter.
Families rush by,
kids squealing with joy,
robes flowing behind
as they run towards
their dreams made real.
Dragons and Wizards.
Aliens and Mummies.
The imagination is opened
with the paint applied
heavily to stucco.
The effects and sounds,
the lights and music,
create bubbles in the brain.
Like the bubbles in my drink.
The Hawaiian patterns on the shirts
match the tunes on the speakers.
Everything is sweet.
Everyone is happy.
I am happy.
It is the happiest place on earth...
according to the **NEON LIGHTS.**

SHE STANDS

Holding my breath.
Trying to not make a sound.
Finger pushing down lightly
against the smooth button.
Click.
Click.
Zoom in.
Click.
I see the deep brown eye,
wise with the years.
Pain and fear reflected
for just a moment
as it flickers towards me
acknowledging the slight sound
that my finger made.
My eye leaves the viewer
to see the beauty
without a pane of mirrored glass between us.
AND THERE SHE STANDS.
A graceful boulder in the world.
Her eyes shift back to the ground,
long eyelashes hiding their knowledge.
Her leathery ears flap slightly
at her side,
causing a halo of bugs to fly up
and circle
before landing again
into the grey folds of her skin.

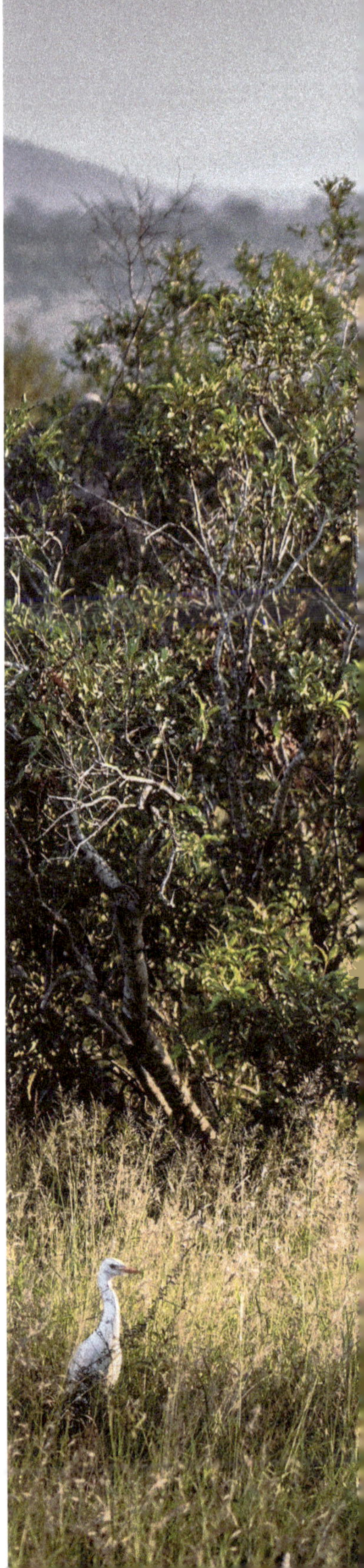

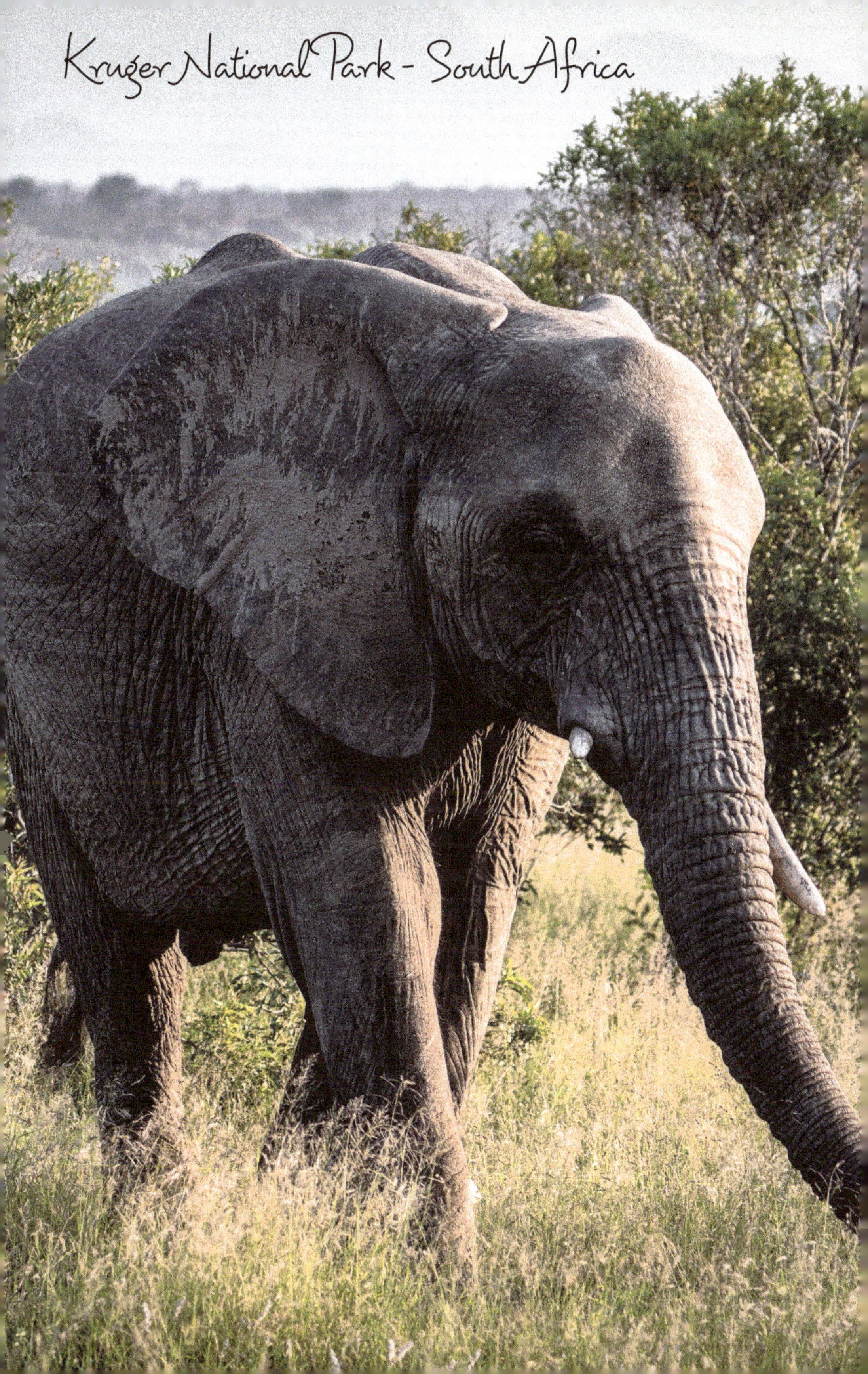
Kruger National Park - South Africa

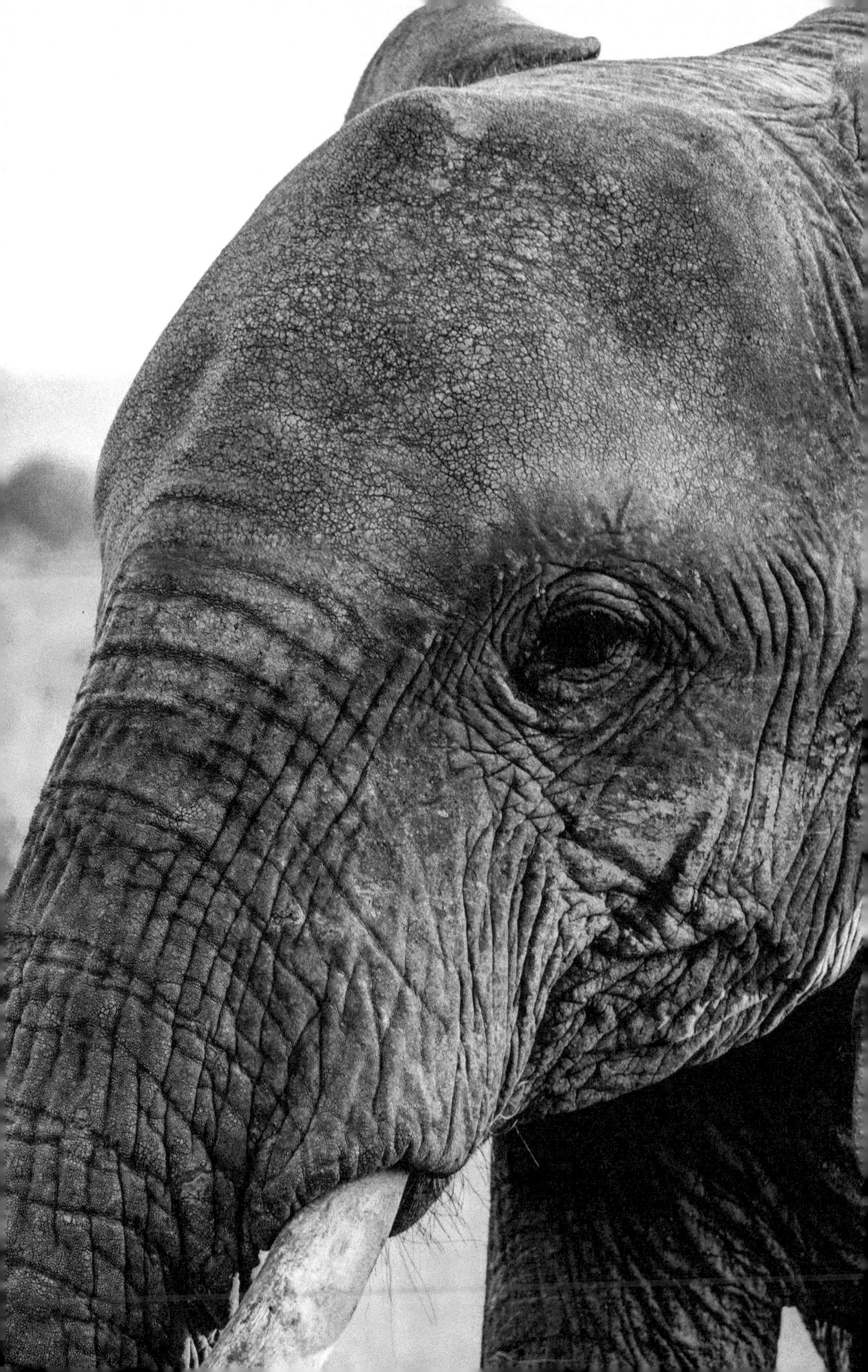

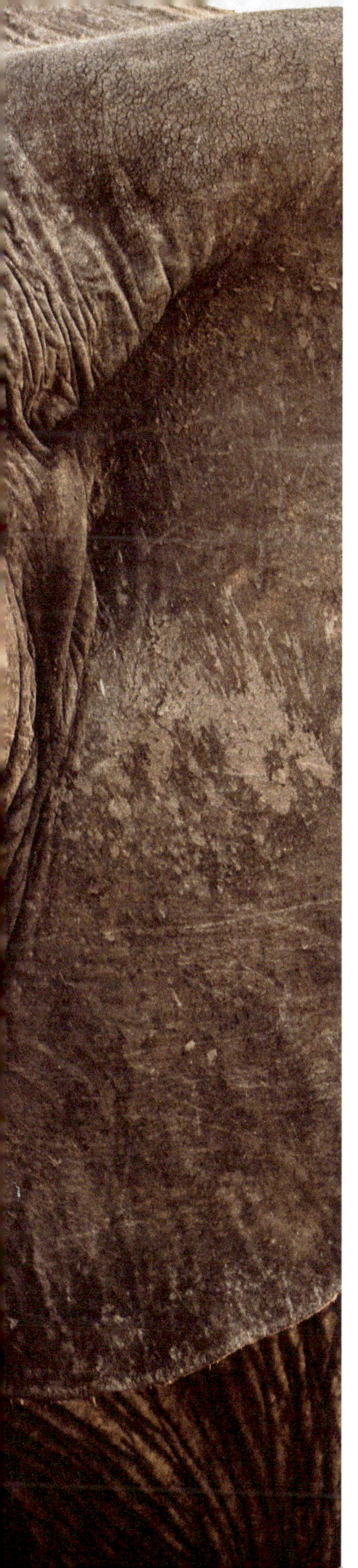

Her trunk feeling along the ground
until its finger finds the gold
and it rises quickly,
bringing dark mud with it,
splashing against her skin
to keep her cool
under the hot
burning
African sun.
My skin burns too
as I sit
not wanting to move from this spot.
From this moment.
This magical second
that could be eternity.
She turns with grace,
deciding I'm no threat,
and takes a lingering step
away from me.
White birds flow in her wake,
the unabashed excitement
at the new bugs that
her lumbering feet reveal.
I watch with wonder,
honored to share this moment.
I lift the camera to my eye.

CLICK.

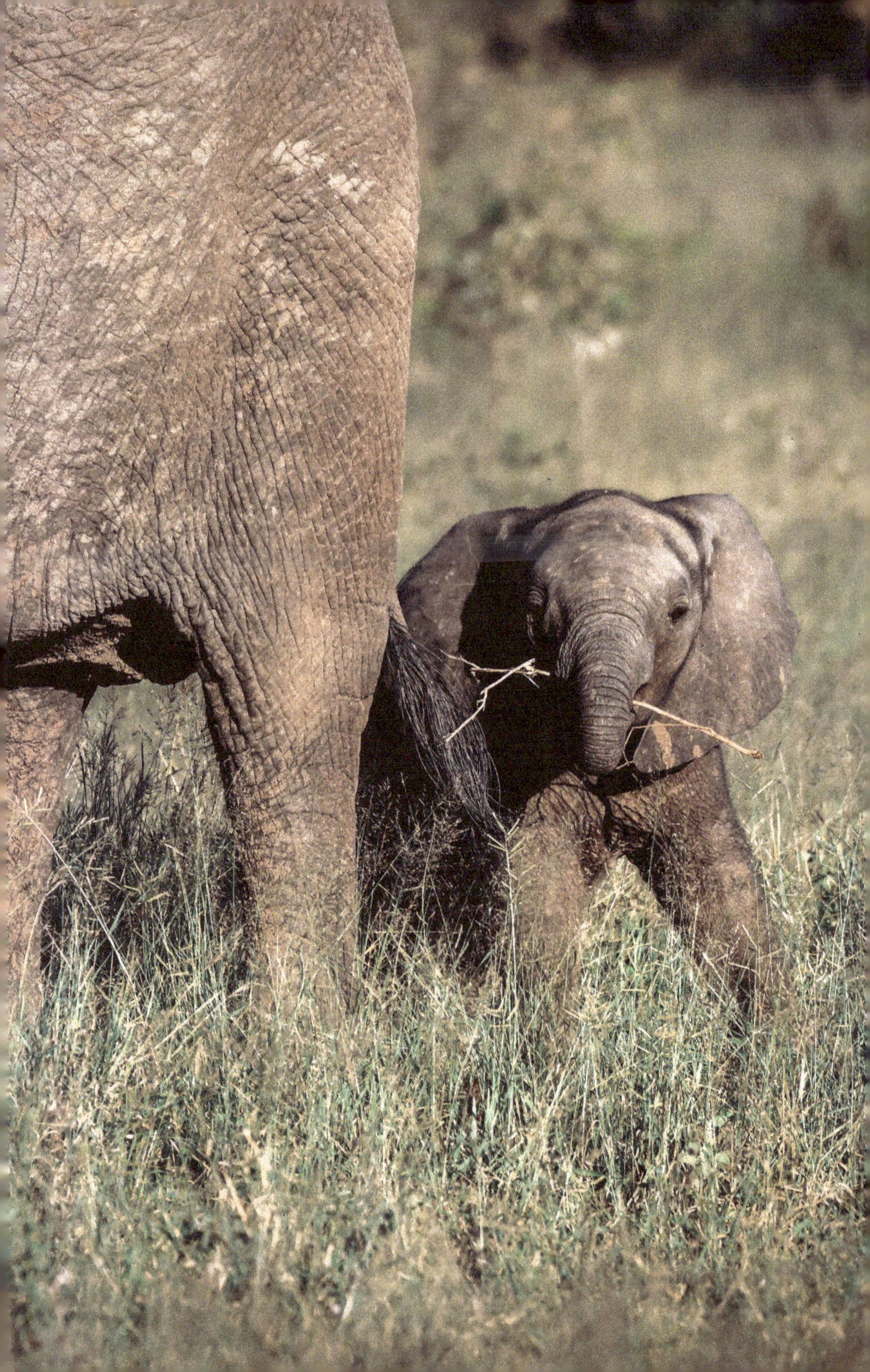

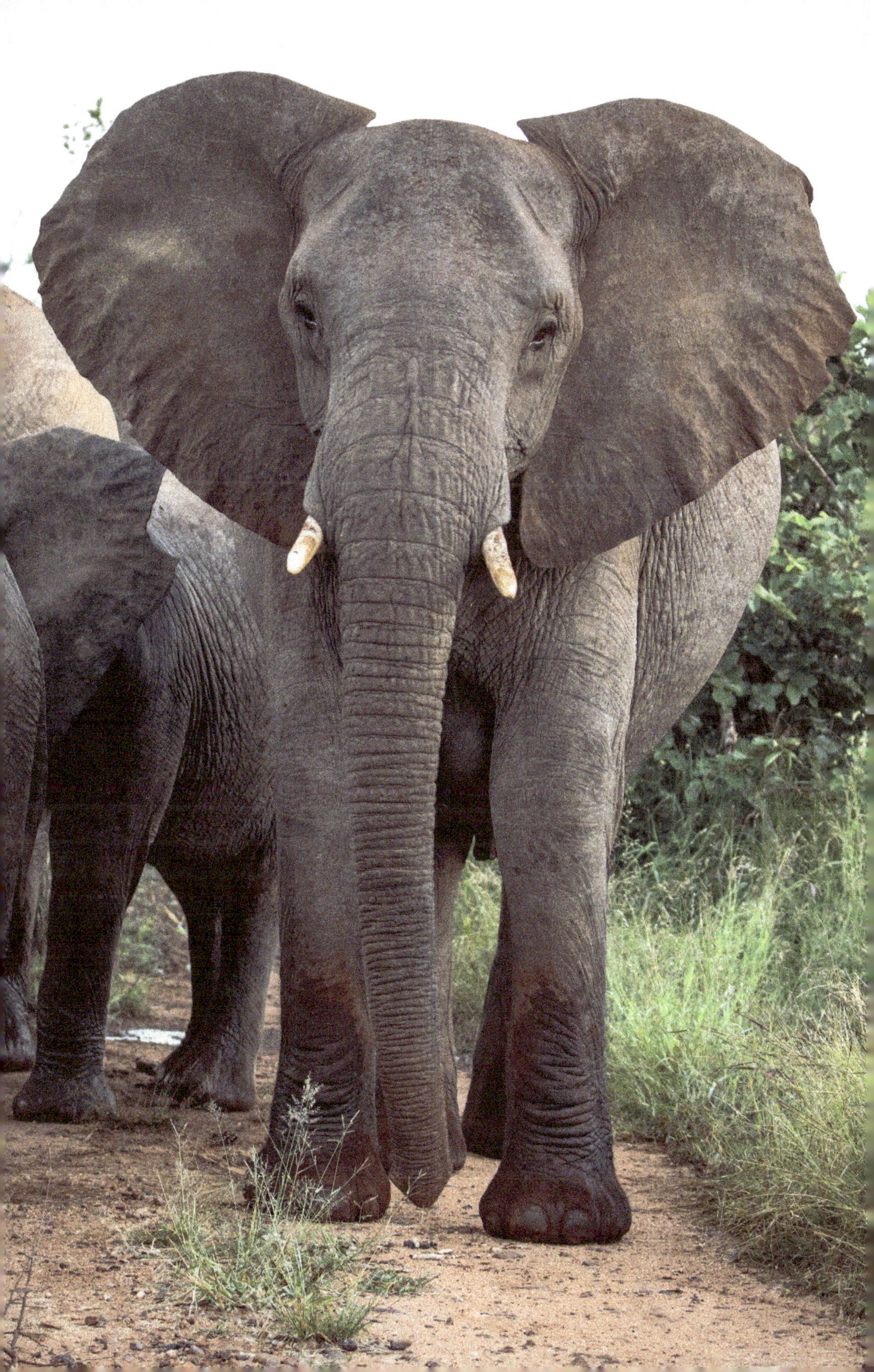

GREEK SOUL

No screens.
No distractions.
Everyone lost in conversation.
Laughing.
Smiling.
Halfway across the globe
people are rushing and sweating
but here that's never a thought.
Sit.
Relax.
Converse.
Let the air thick with fish and salt
fill your lungs.
Breathe in the lingering odors
of fresh coffee and crisp cheese.
Let the noon drink flow down your throat
stinging so sweetly.
A cat brushes past your leg.
A donkey whinnies across the
cobblestone path.
No cars.
No pollution.
Everyone is your friend...
or if they aren't, they soon will be.
Feel as every muscle relaxes.
The sun warms your soul
and the seat you are in
as it lowers behind the hill.
The ancient buildings climb the hillside.
The fishing boats roll in.
Everyone yelling greetings
in this daily life
built on a rock
sticking out of the sea.
Do I belong here?
I think so.

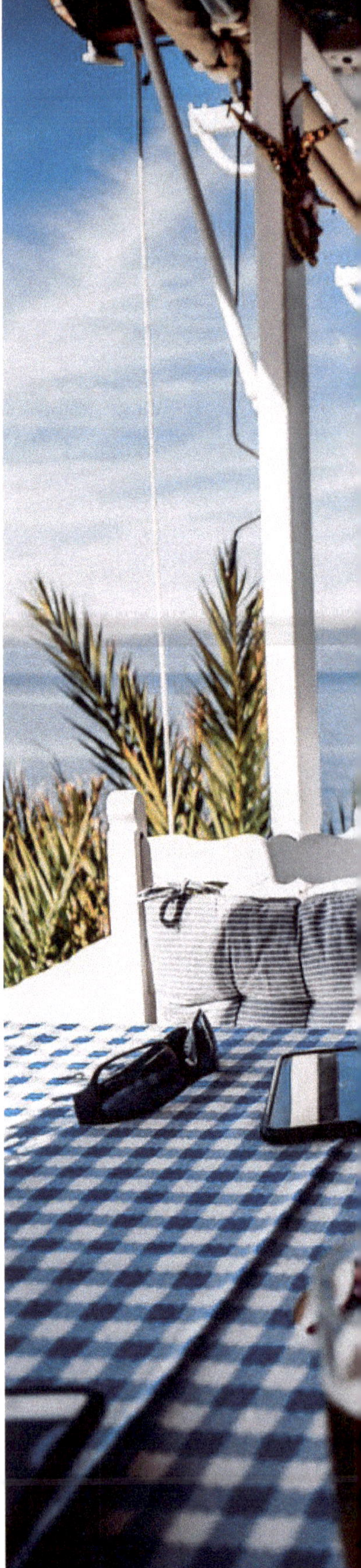

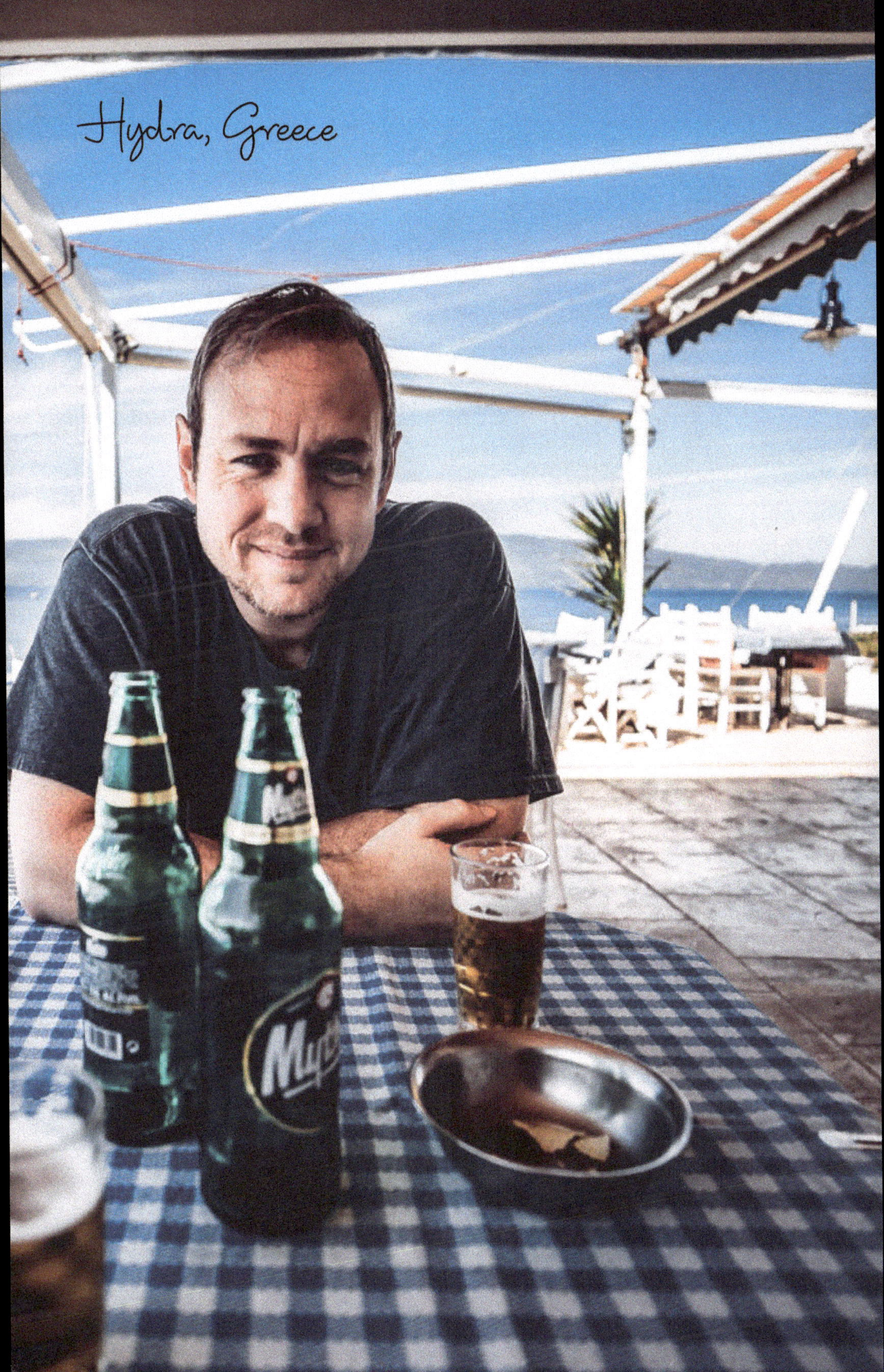
Hydra, Greece

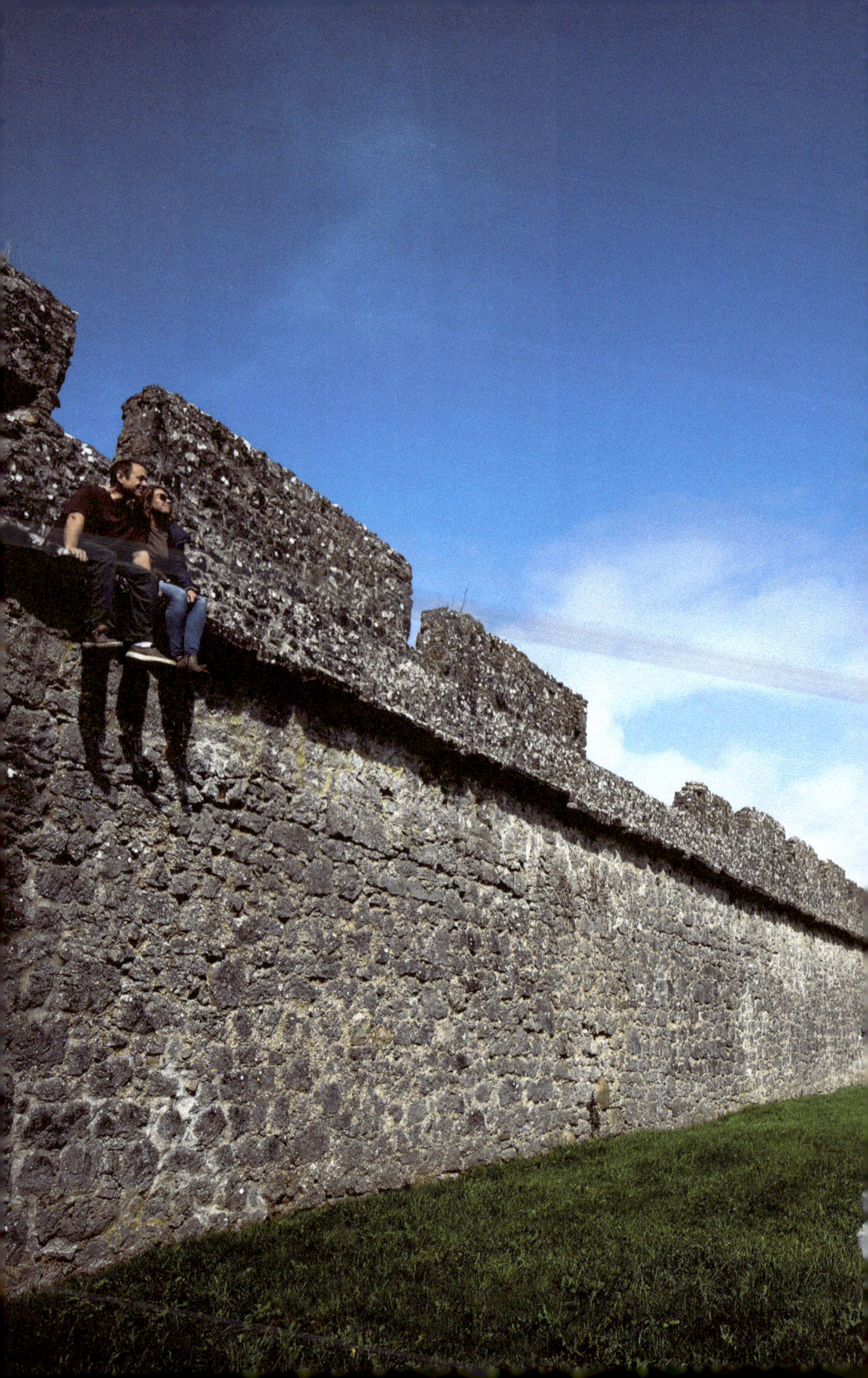

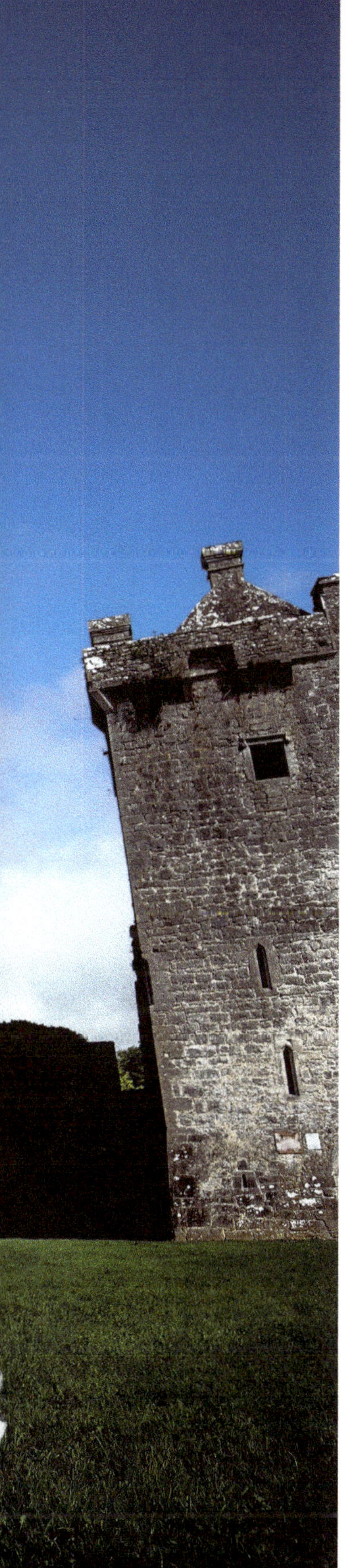

WHEN IN IRELAND

A castle hidden in the woods
Nowhere near other neighborhoods
The grass was lush and green
Mowed recently it seemed
As they also trimmed the dogwoods

Drove one way down a one-way road
As we neared the stone walls, we slowed.
No other souls in sight
The sun was shining bright
When we found the ancient abode

There wasn't a sound in the day
As we shimmied through the gateway
Into the green courtyard
Feeling like a vanguard
Exploring alone 'til midday

The stone walls told stories of past
Wonderment, of how this will outlast
As others fall away
This one is here to stay
Hidden far away from Belfast

We climbed the wall and sat 'til late
Broken stone still holding our weight
Thinking "what came before?"
Picturing all the lore
Wish we could stay behind this gate

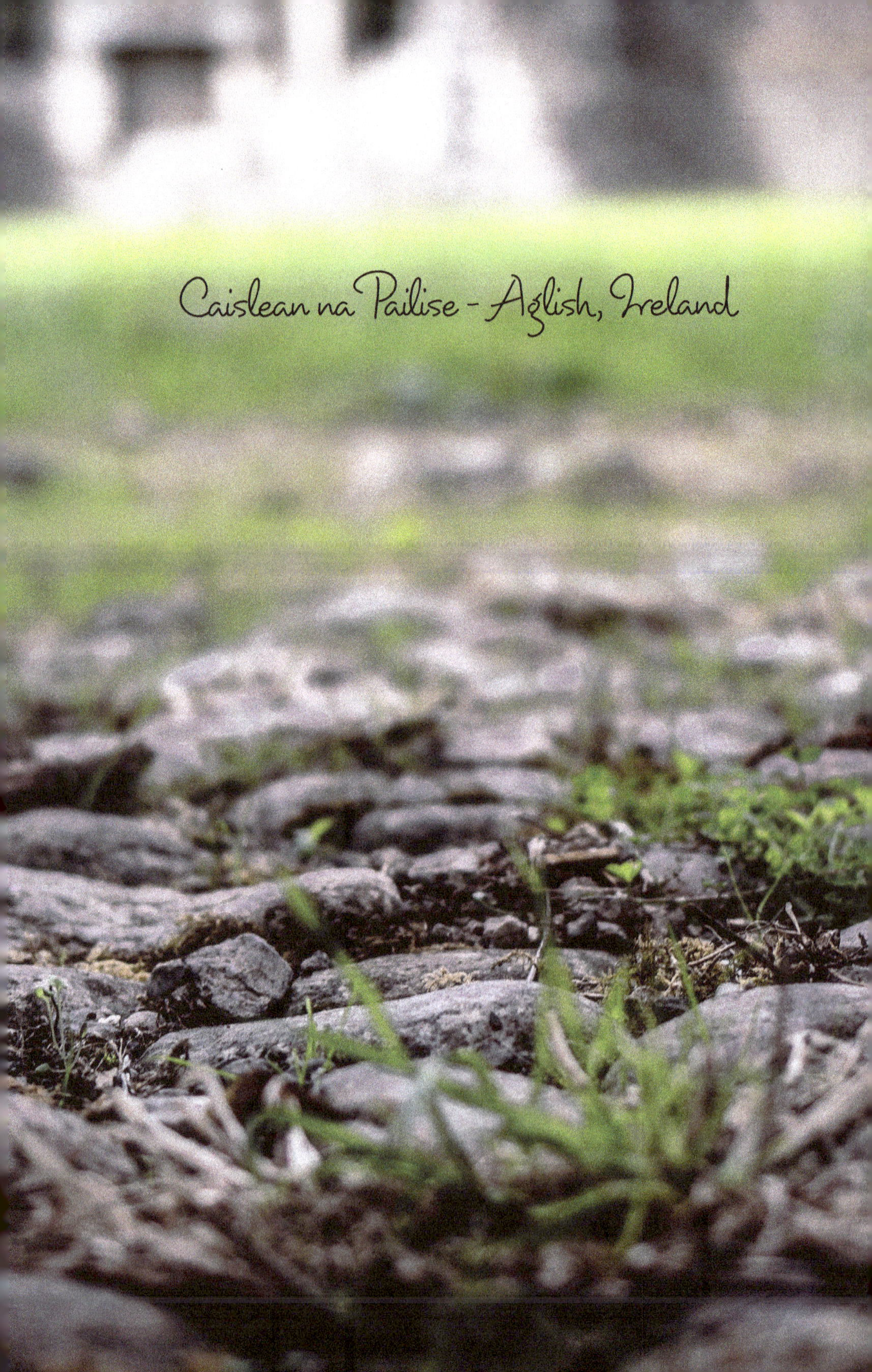
Caislean na Pailise - Aglish, Ireland

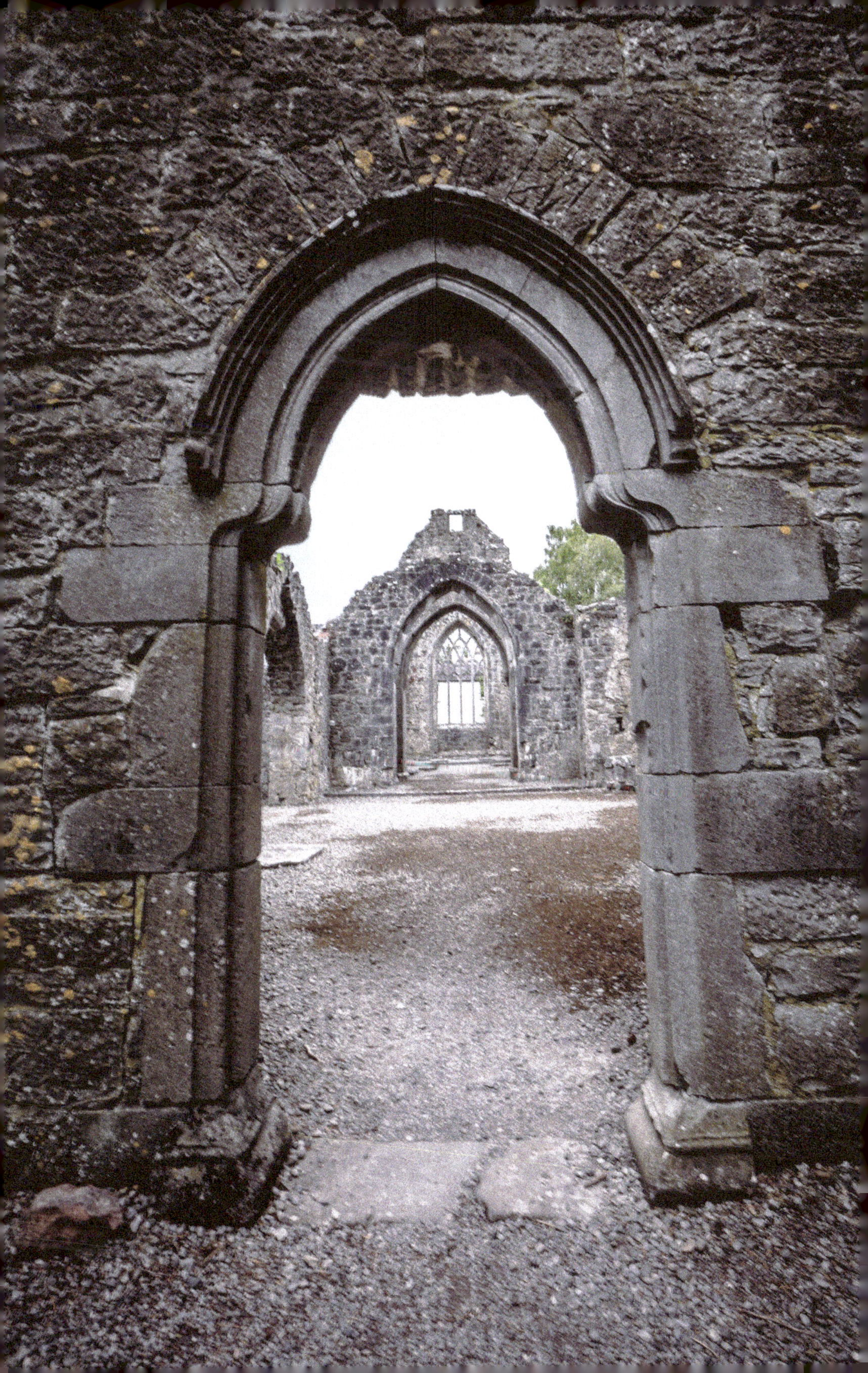

SHE SIGHS

"no one has been here"
the clean snow tells us
as it crunches beneath our feet
no one has been here except us
the explorers
the adventurers
the frozen

no one has been here
there is nothing but soft white
but then our eyes lift
to find the old blue
beneath the new blue of the sky
she shines and beckons
"come to me"

we crunch closer
until the bright blue gap is right there
hovering in front of us
our arms lift
reaching
towards the blue made of life
life that has been
life that has yet to be
she is the beginning
and the end

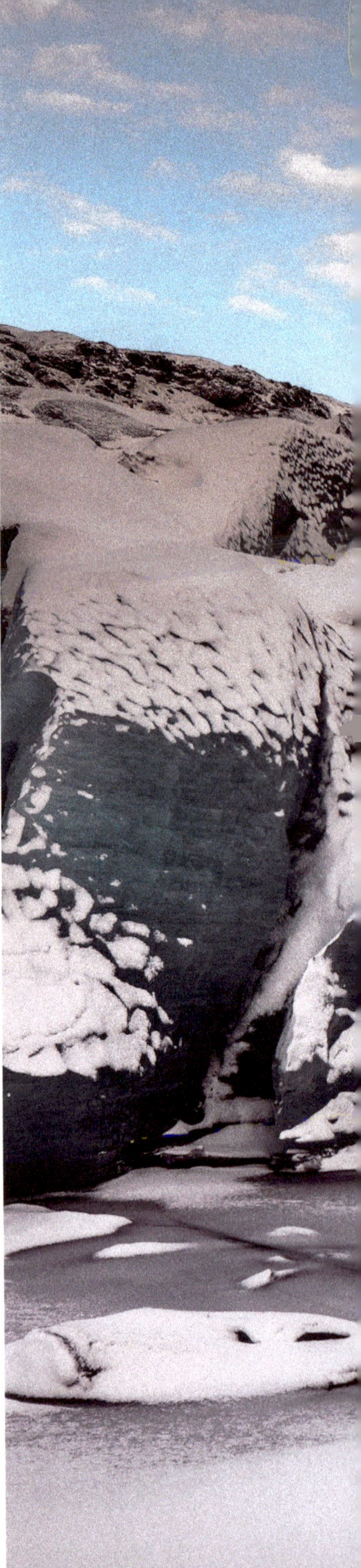

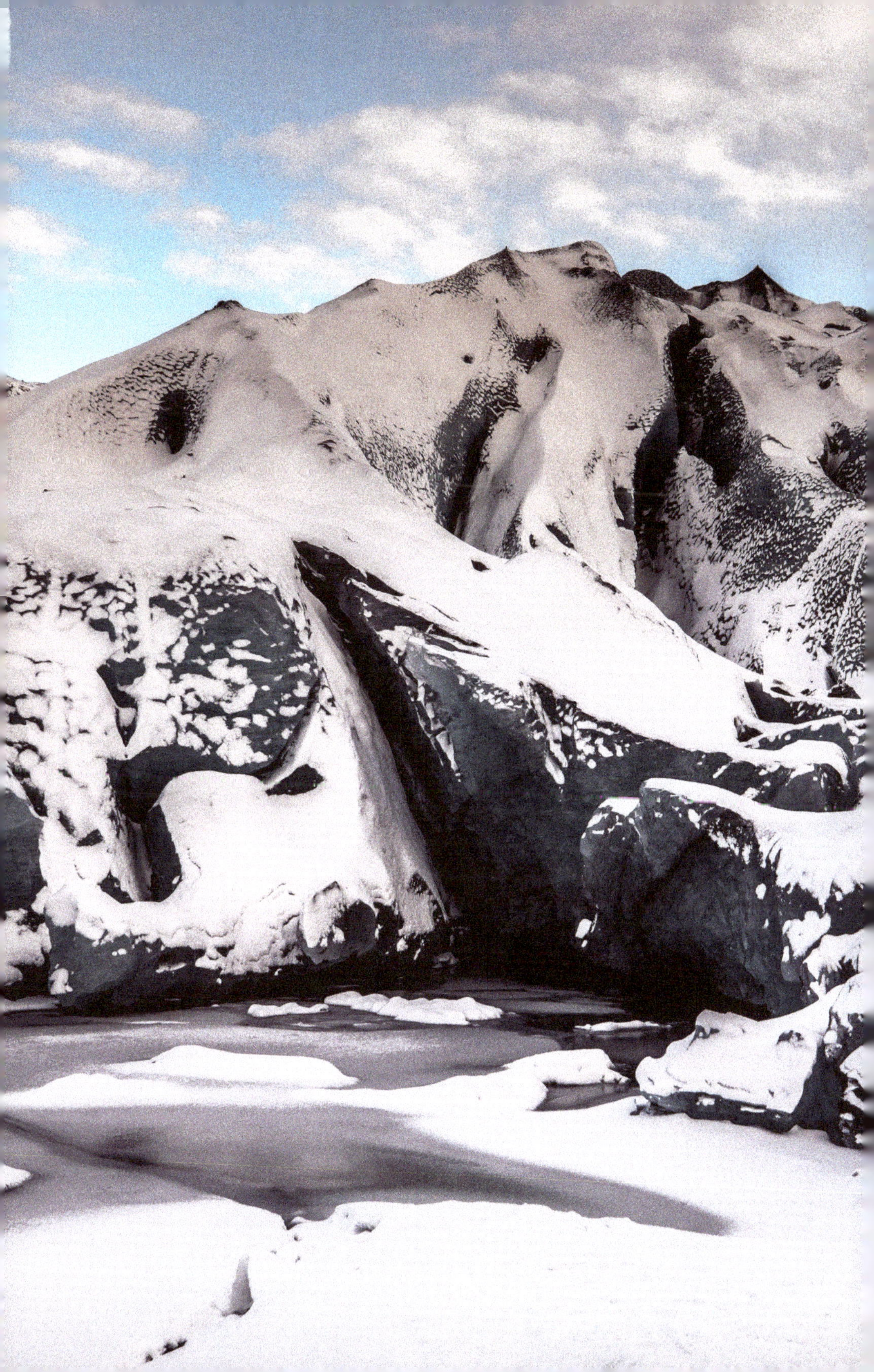

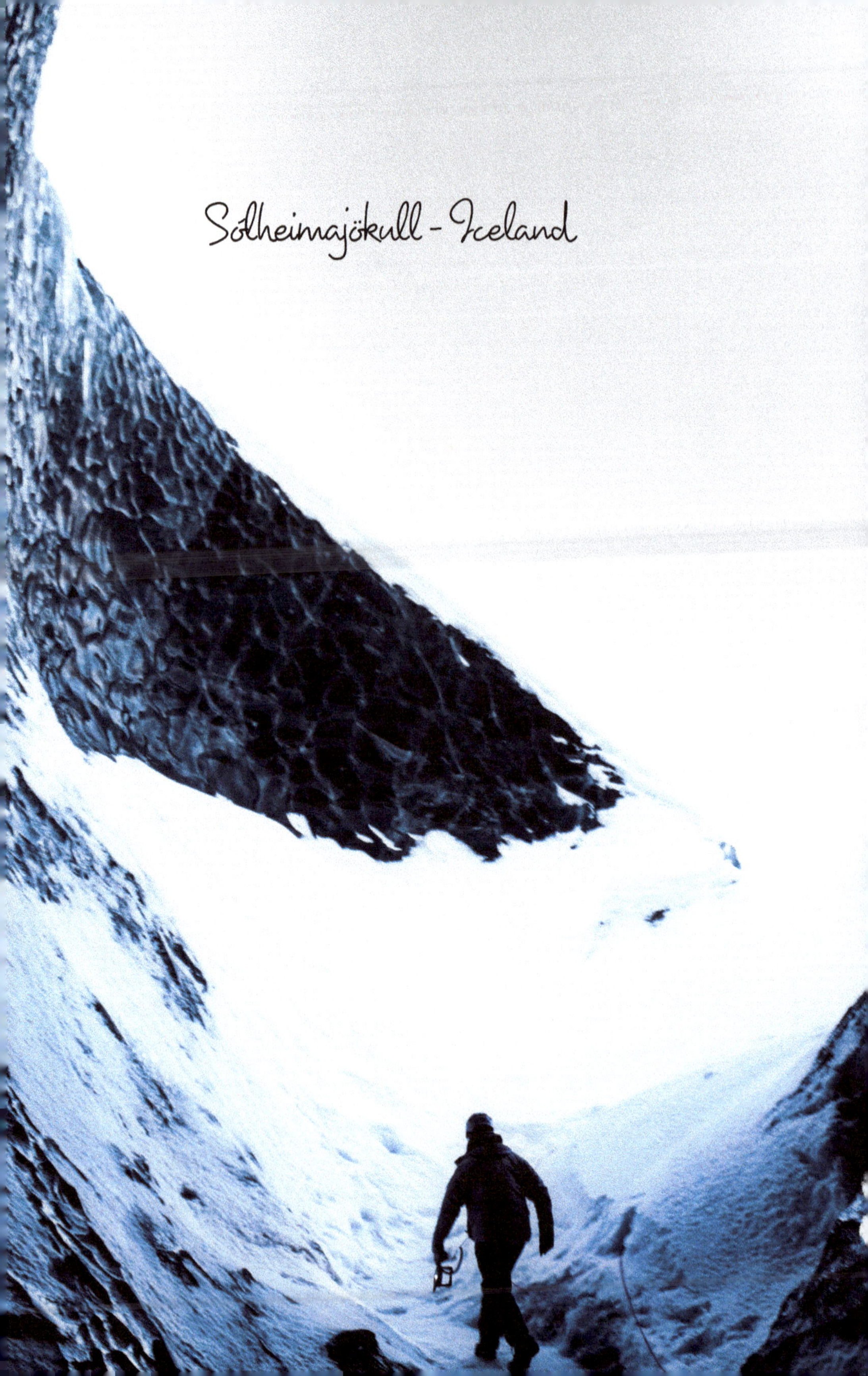
Sólheimajökull - Iceland

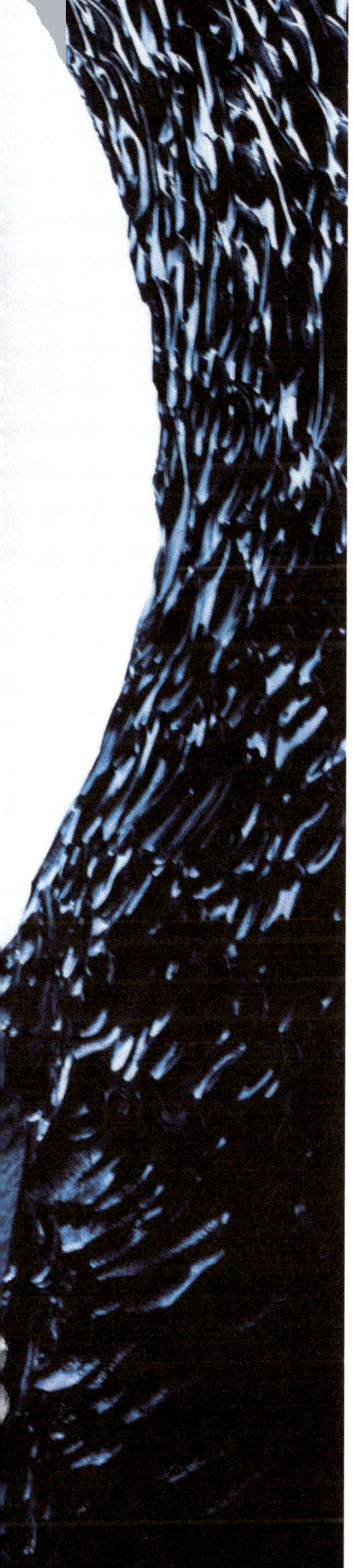

there is no sound
but the crunch beneath us
and the drip
drip
drip
of the melting blue ice
crying for the future

our fingers caress her side
in comfort and awe
smooth and soft to the touch
she feels beautiful
she feels...
everything

she reaches above our heads
a quiet blue cave
the light from our helmets reflects
every dark corner shines
sharing her secrets

our collective breath slows
as we take in each moment
that we are standing in
the history
the power
the magic
of the ancient blue cave
as she sighs under the weight of the snow

PAINTED RED

Legs pushing
Pulsating
Peddling
Eyes starring
Down at the pavement below
And in front
Focusing
Moving
Slowly

Paused
Catching breath
Eyes drift
Up
Up
Up
Pavement gives way
To steel painted red
Red erecting out of blue
Protruding against deep green
Cars fly past
Lost in their own worlds
So am I
Lost in my world
Seeing
Understanding
Experiencing
The beauty I'm standing on
The behemoth of red
Taken for granted
On daily commutes
Connecting two sides
Multiple worlds
Powerful and bright
Against the monotone land beneath
Providing a path
A connection
With steel
Simply painted red

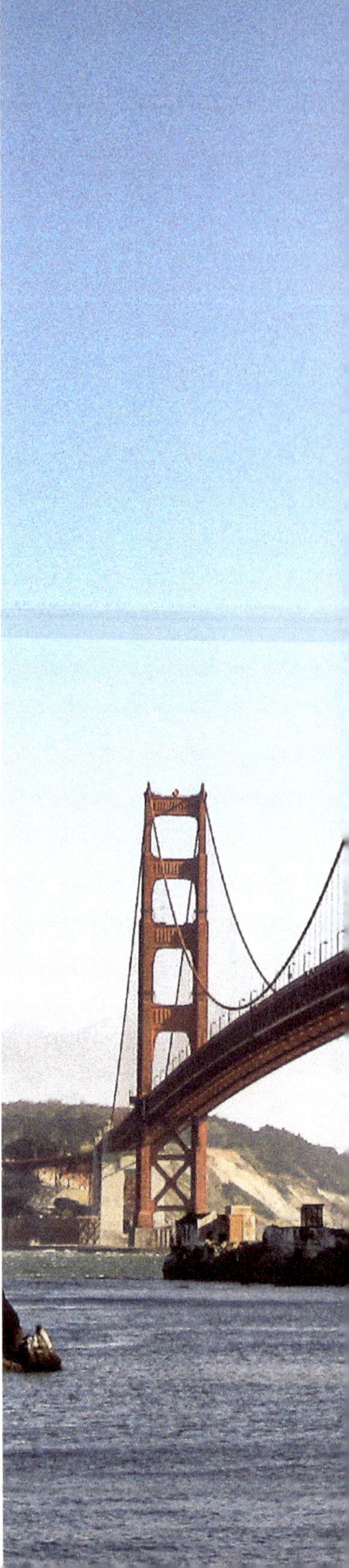

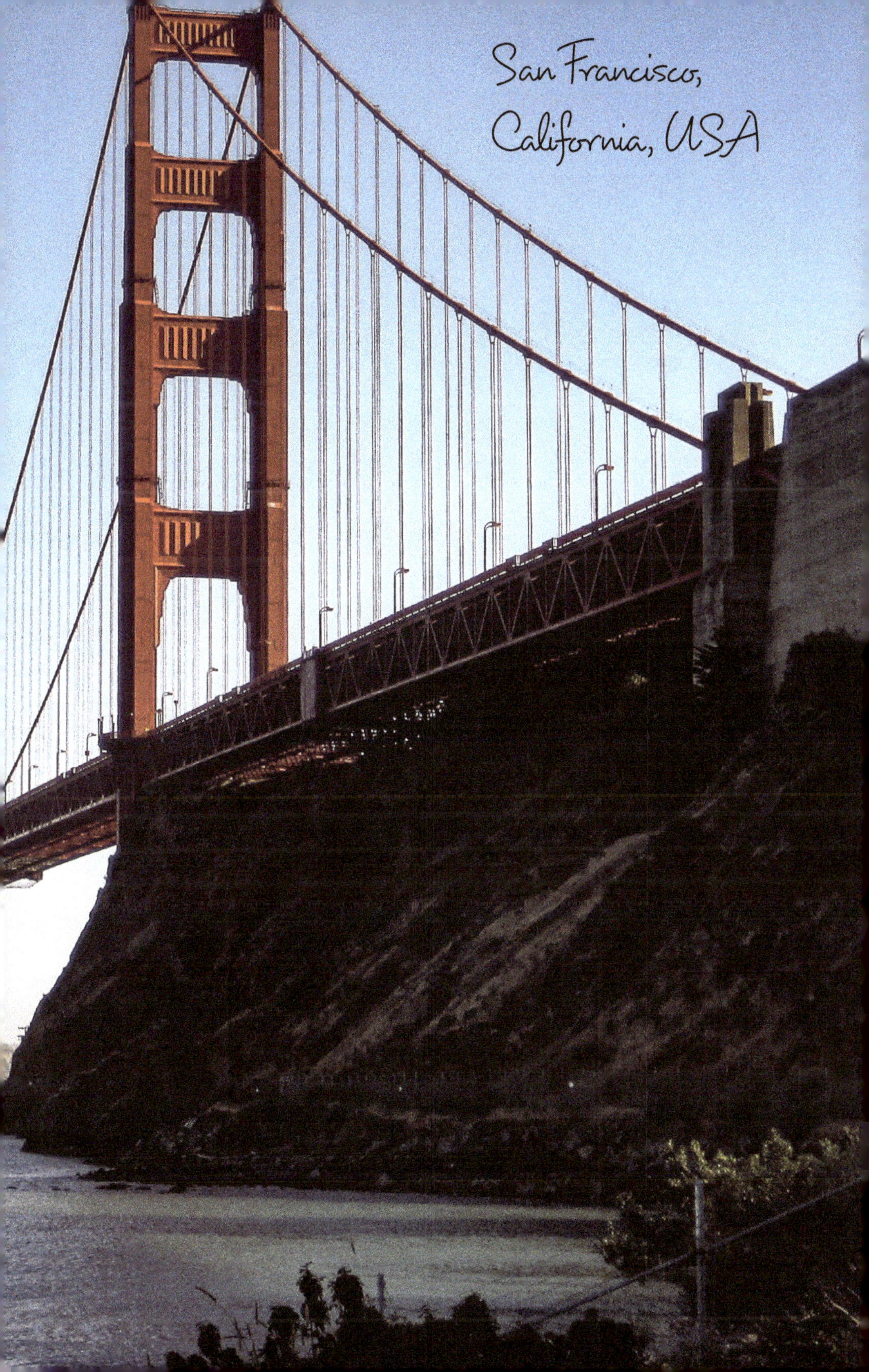
San Francisco,
California, USA

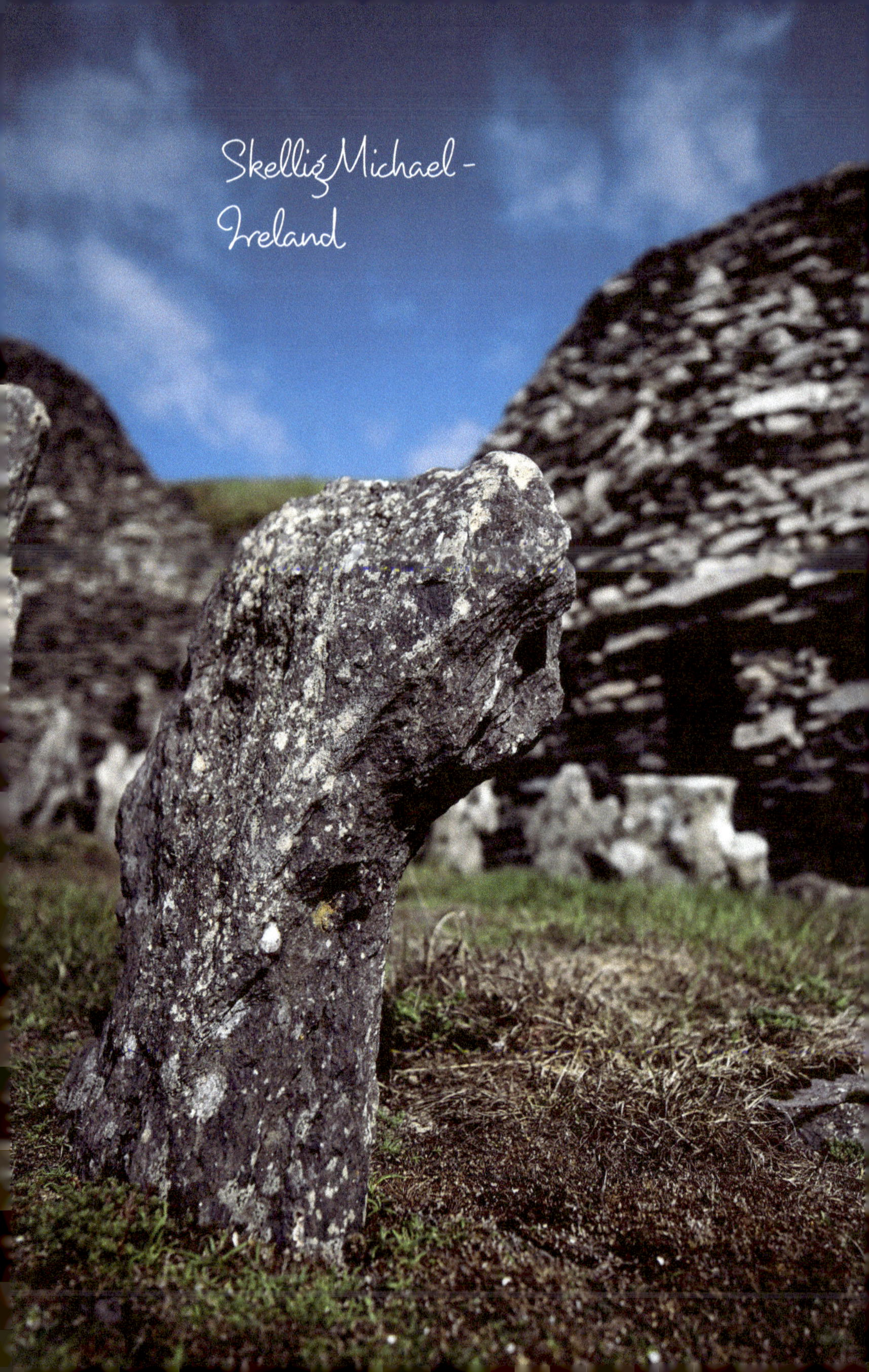
Skellig Michael -
Ireland

SIX HUNDRED STEPS

Six hundred steps
built into the side
of a beautiful green rock
that juts out of the raging sea.
Steps made of stone
and slate
climbed hundreds of years ago
by the men who built them
away from persecution.
Driven to this magnificent island
that juts out of the sea.
Climb up the steps
built into the rocks.
To see.
To share.
Climb up
closer to the god
of the monks
who are long dead
and gone.
Their memory alone is built into
their homes.
Beehives made of slate
at the top of this enchanting rock
that juts out of the bottomless sea.
Far in the distance,
another rock,
sharp and steep.
The brother to our own.
Further still,
the mother.
The land
clouded by sea fog
and mysticism
that mirrors that
of the monks of old
who built the steps of slate
to climb closer to god
on this beautiful green island
that juts out of the deep blue sea.

"PLEASE BROTHER"

"please brother"
His eyes are pleading
begging
as his wife pushes him forward
his wheelchair banging
against the bright orange rickshaw
where a stranger sits ignoring
the thin arms stretched for a coin
that never comes

"please brother"
The only request he knows
his legs lost just at the knee
he clings to his seat
and clutches his metal plate to his chest
his chair bouncing
against the broken pavement below
as they speed towards the line
to wait for their rations

"please brother"
He coughs from behind his scarf
pulled up to his nose
protecting his face
from the heavy clouds
of grime and dirt and smog
as it weighs down
against his frail shoulders
as heavy as the starvation

"please brother"
He whispers toward the fruit
his eyes barely able
to meet the gaze of the man standing
there behind the table
watching him wearily
the frail man thinks of his children
and raises his arms
imploring with the only words he can

"please brother"

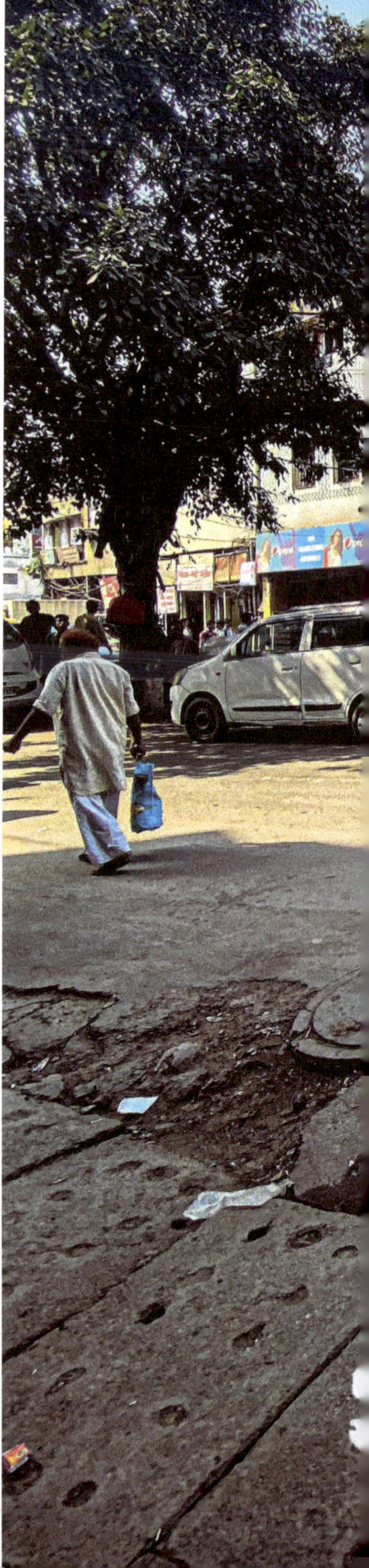

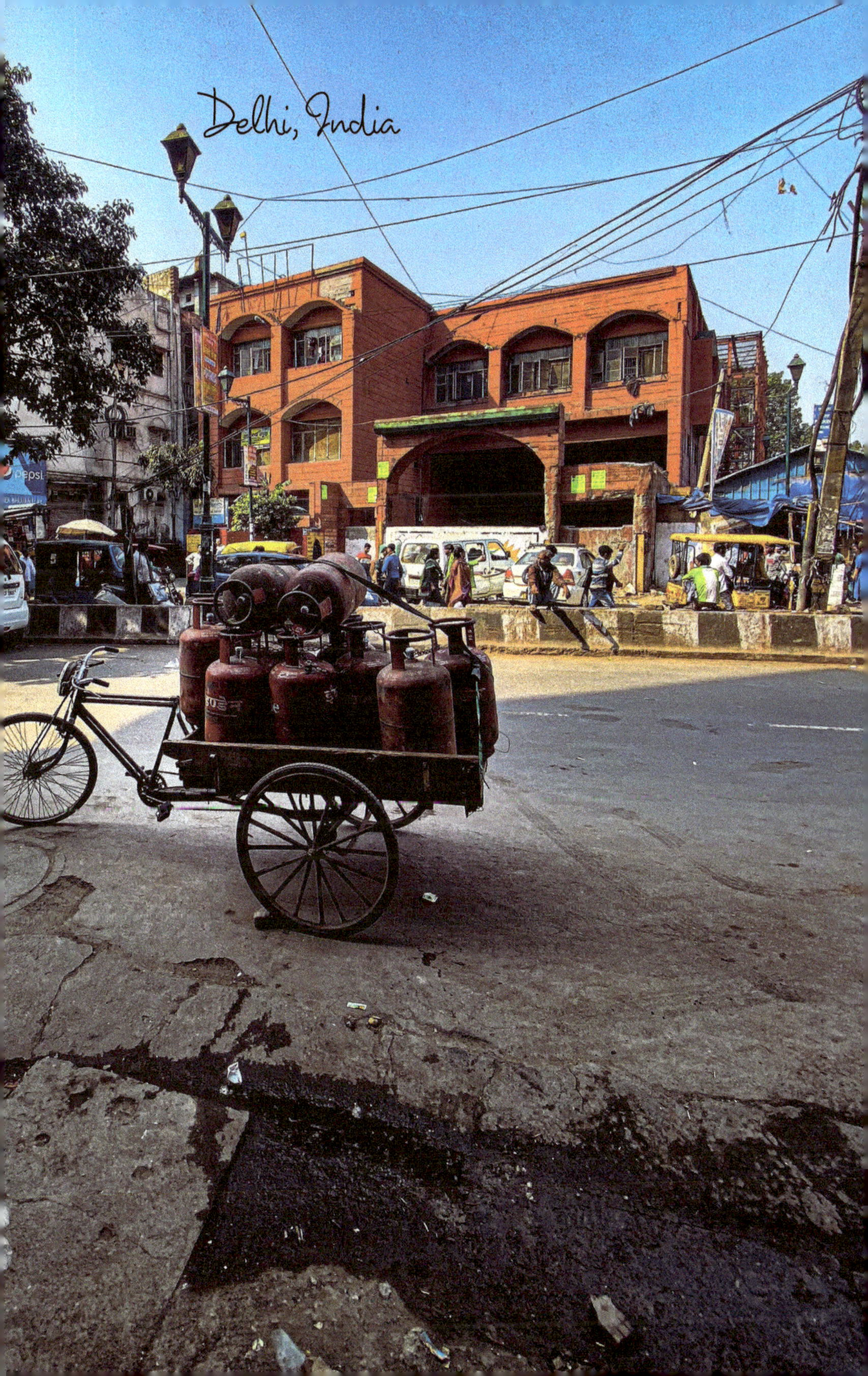
Delhi, India

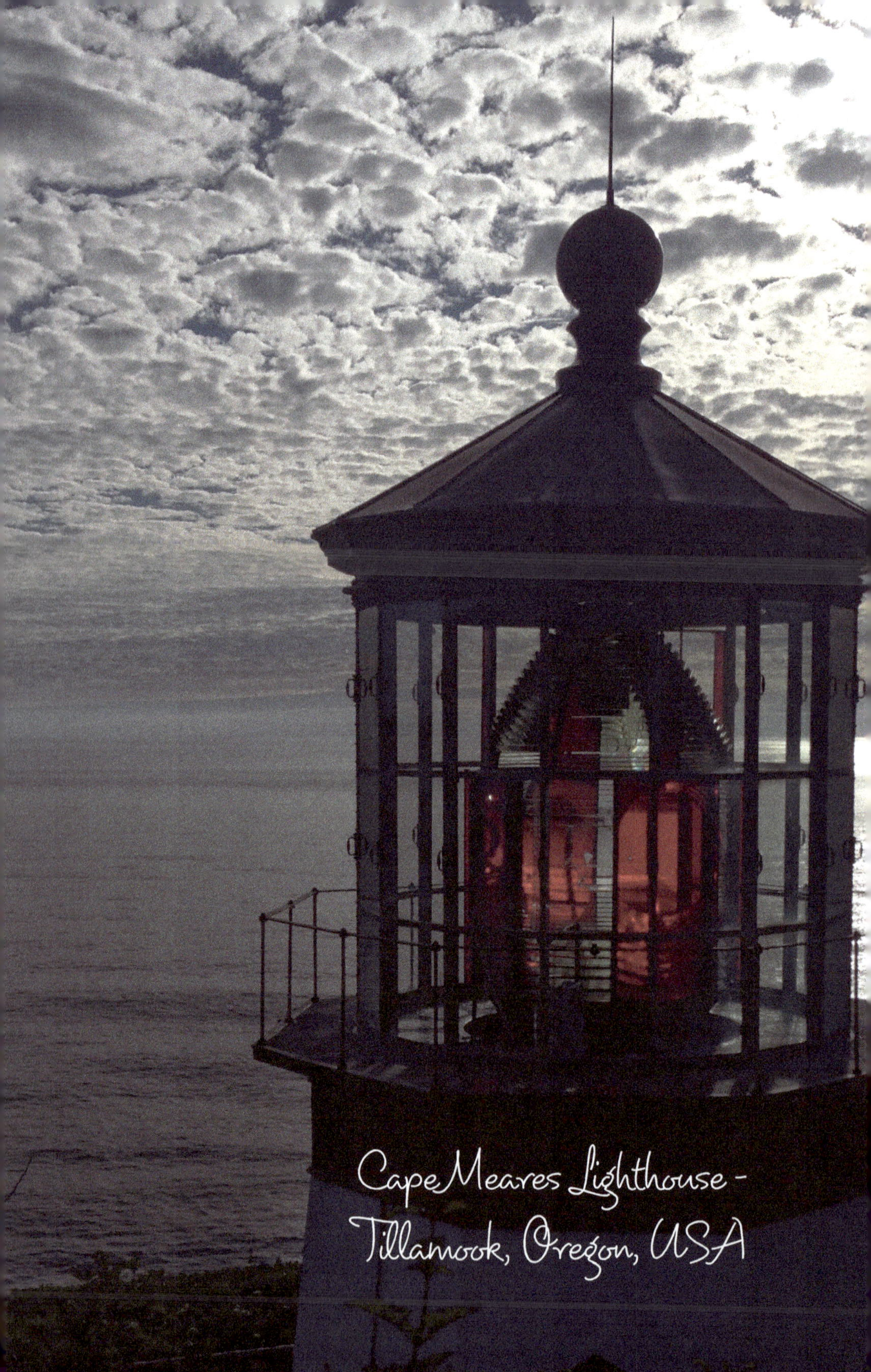
Cape Meares Lighthouse -
Tillamook, Oregon, USA

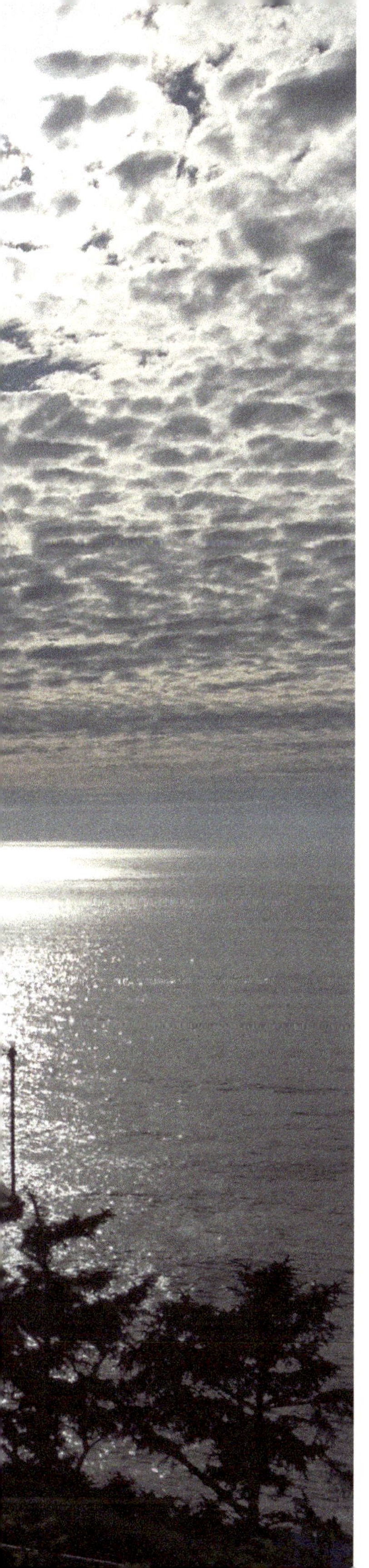

THE LIGHT

Cool wind blows
The storm rolls in
Coming from the distant blue wall
The light turns towards the land
My eyes close
And I stand
In the place they used to stand
The men
And the women
Who guided the sailors home
What became of them?
The sailors
And their guides
Alone together
Living to see the other
The light coming from a distant soul
Steady on the land
Or moving in the sea
Strong against the storms
Weathered against the difficulties
The loneliness
The quiet nights
And days
Now only stories
Whispered in the wind
As the storm rolls in
And the light turns to the sea

TO GUIDE THE SAILORS HOME

Machias Seal Island
Canada + USA

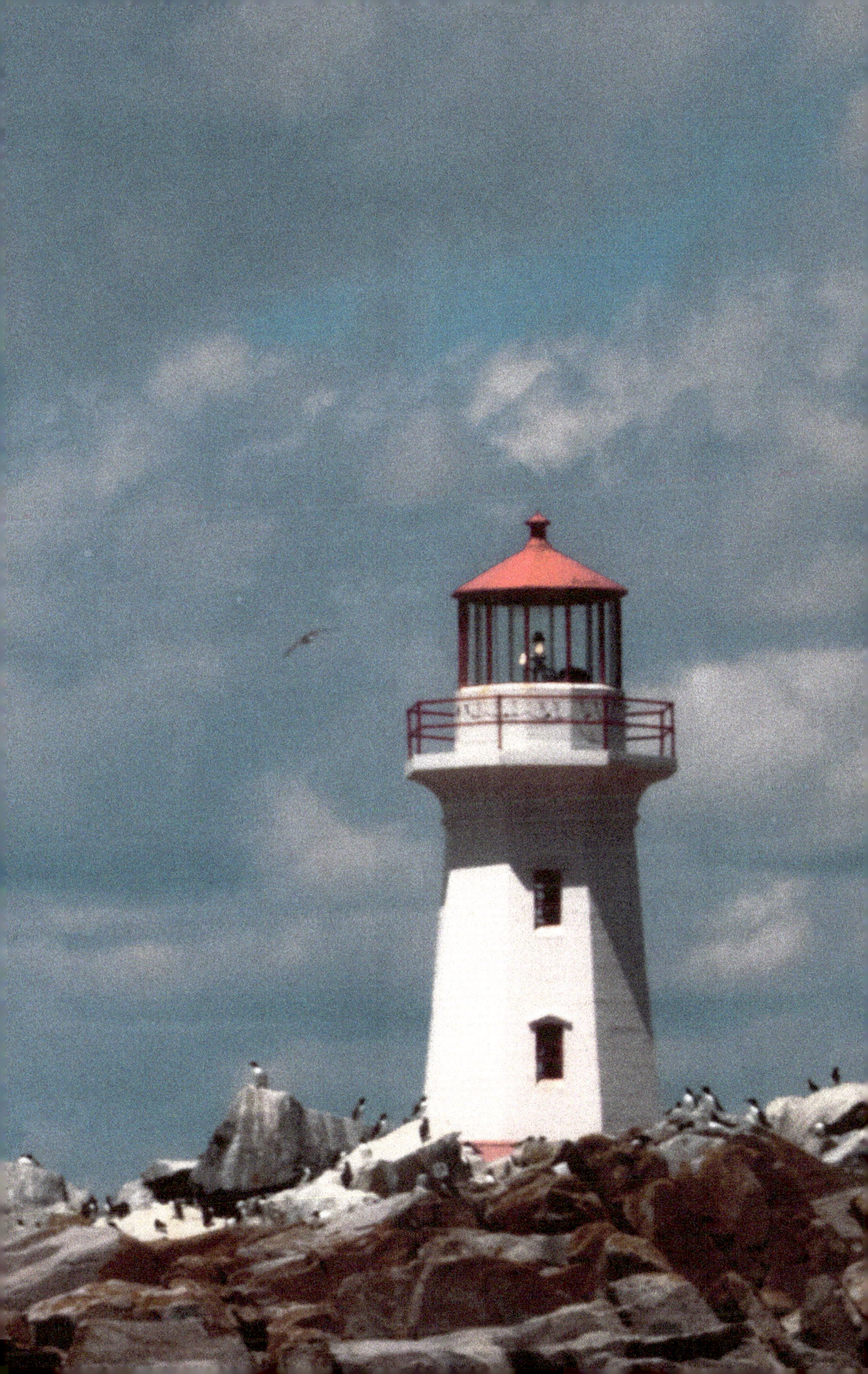

ONE LAST JOURNEY

A woman ***wails***,
the sound cutting through the chaos,
stopping time
as people freeze,
their own mourning on pause.
They rush to the side of the mother
saying goodbye to her son.
The cries fade.
Other sounds fill the air
as another procession continues.
The body wrapped in sunlight
carried to a stone
that still has dust
of gold
from the last adornment.
The body dampened with the water
pulled from the river below
and the sunlight
transforms to orange
as the family blesses him
for his last journey.
Smoke fills the air
from another body
further down the river
already burning
blessed by the water
of the holy river.
The mother ***reaches*** towards
the wrapped body
of her son,
and the people watch
this daily routine
at the Yamuna river
as her wails return
to fill the air
and her son rides them home.

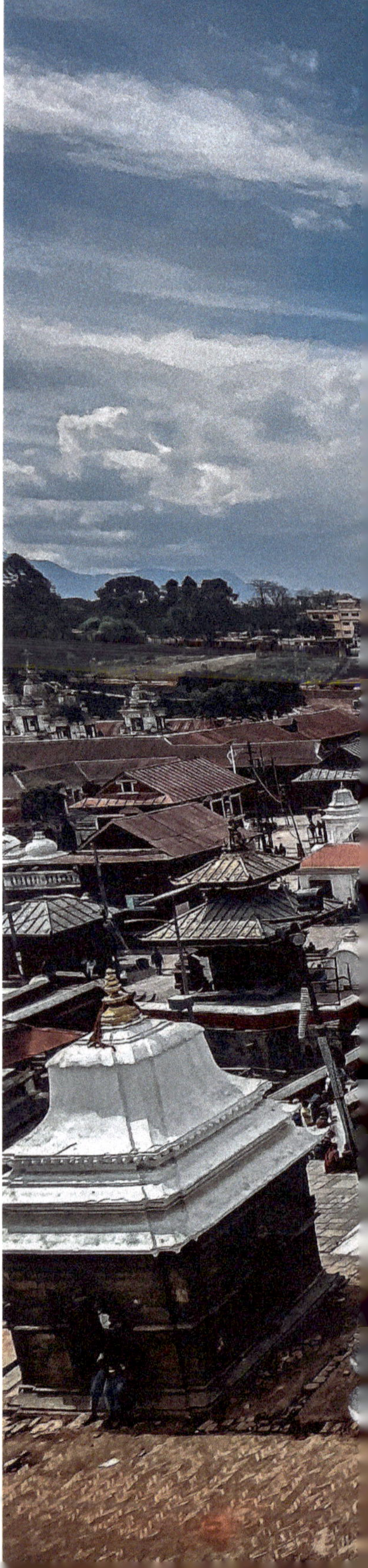

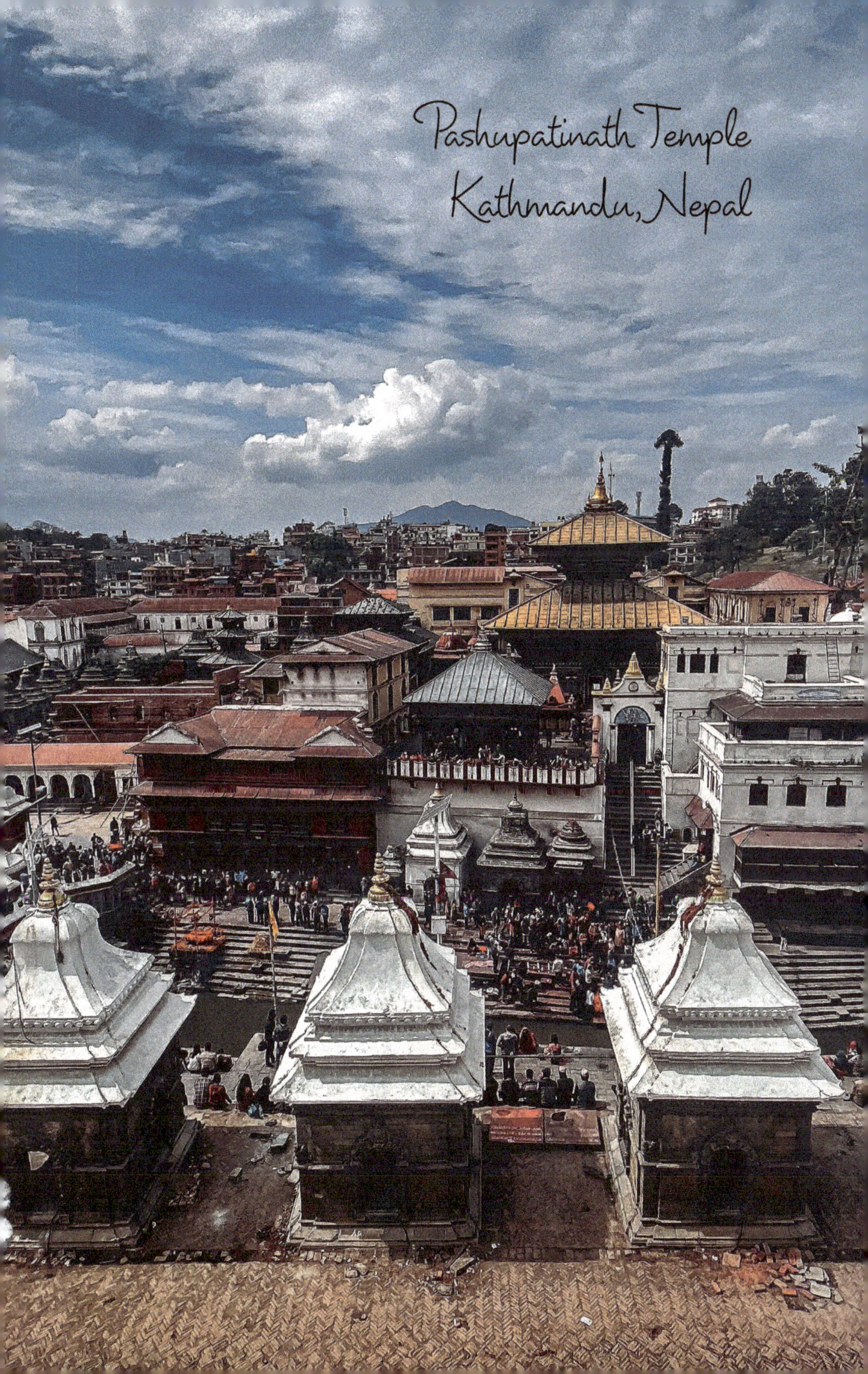
Pashupatinath Temple
Kathmandu, Nepal

HIDDEN

Did you know?
This place where we sit
taking a break
a breath
from walking up
a steep street
on this little bench
burrowed into a wall
put here by someone
knowing that we wouldn't make it
up the steep street
without a break
a breath

Did you know?
That this place has a dark past
a past filled with flame
and death
and when that happened
they built more on top
and buried the old history
trying to forget

Did you know?
It couldn't be forgotten
because the new build
the new grade
of the steep street
caused more pain
and stench
than what the fire left behind
as sewage ran
down the steep street
that we now struggle
to walk up

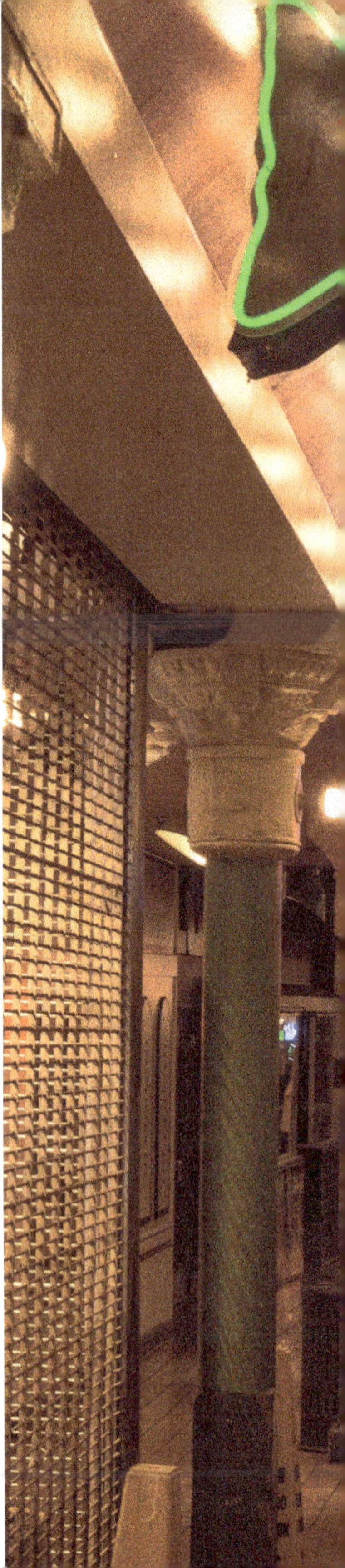

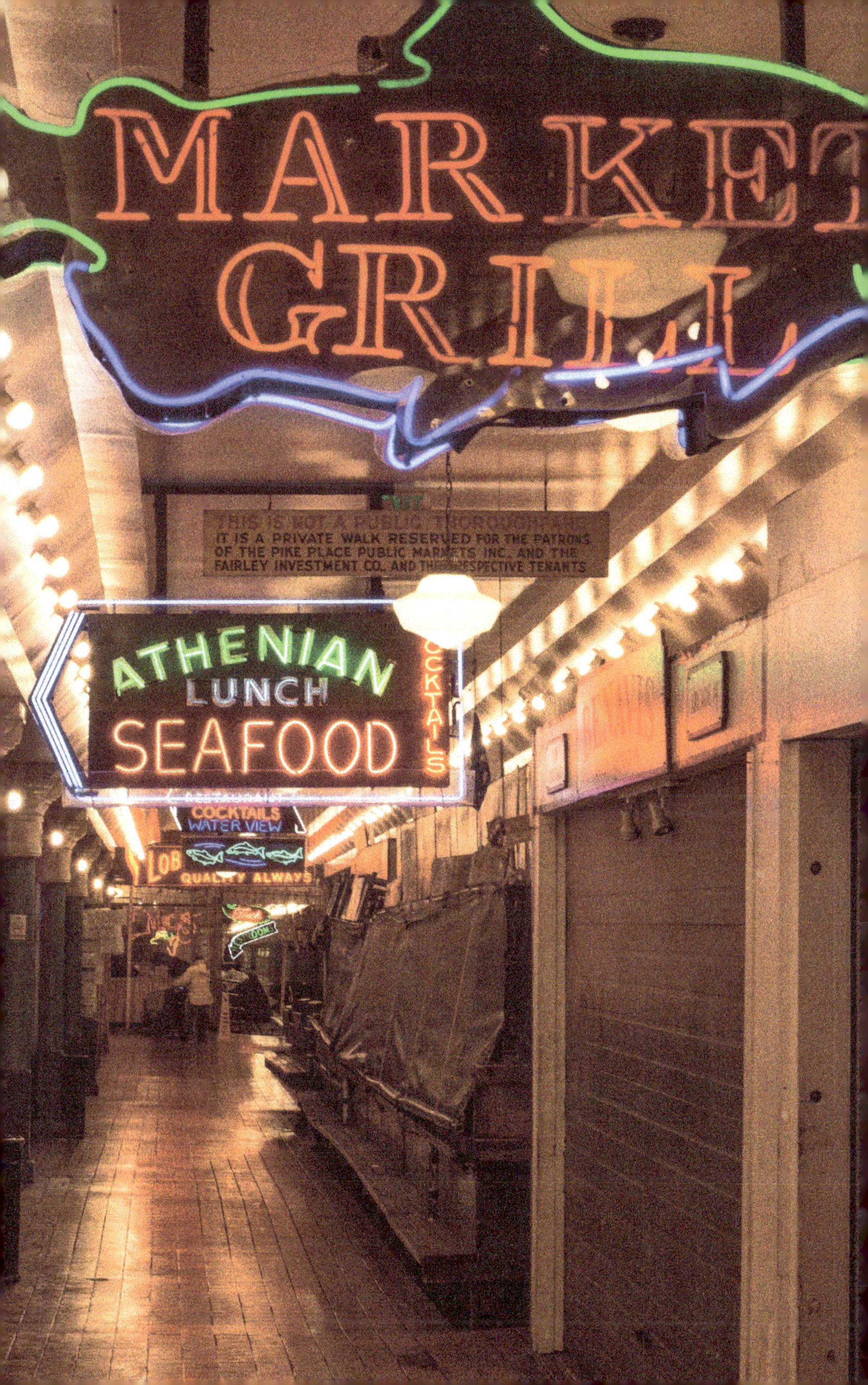

MARKET
GRILL

IT IS A PRIVATE WALK RESERVED FOR THE PATRONS
OF THE PIKE PLACE PUBLIC MARKETS INC. AND THE

ATHENIAN
LUNCH
SEAFOOD
COCKTAILS

COCKTAILS
WATER VIEW

QUALITY ALWAYS

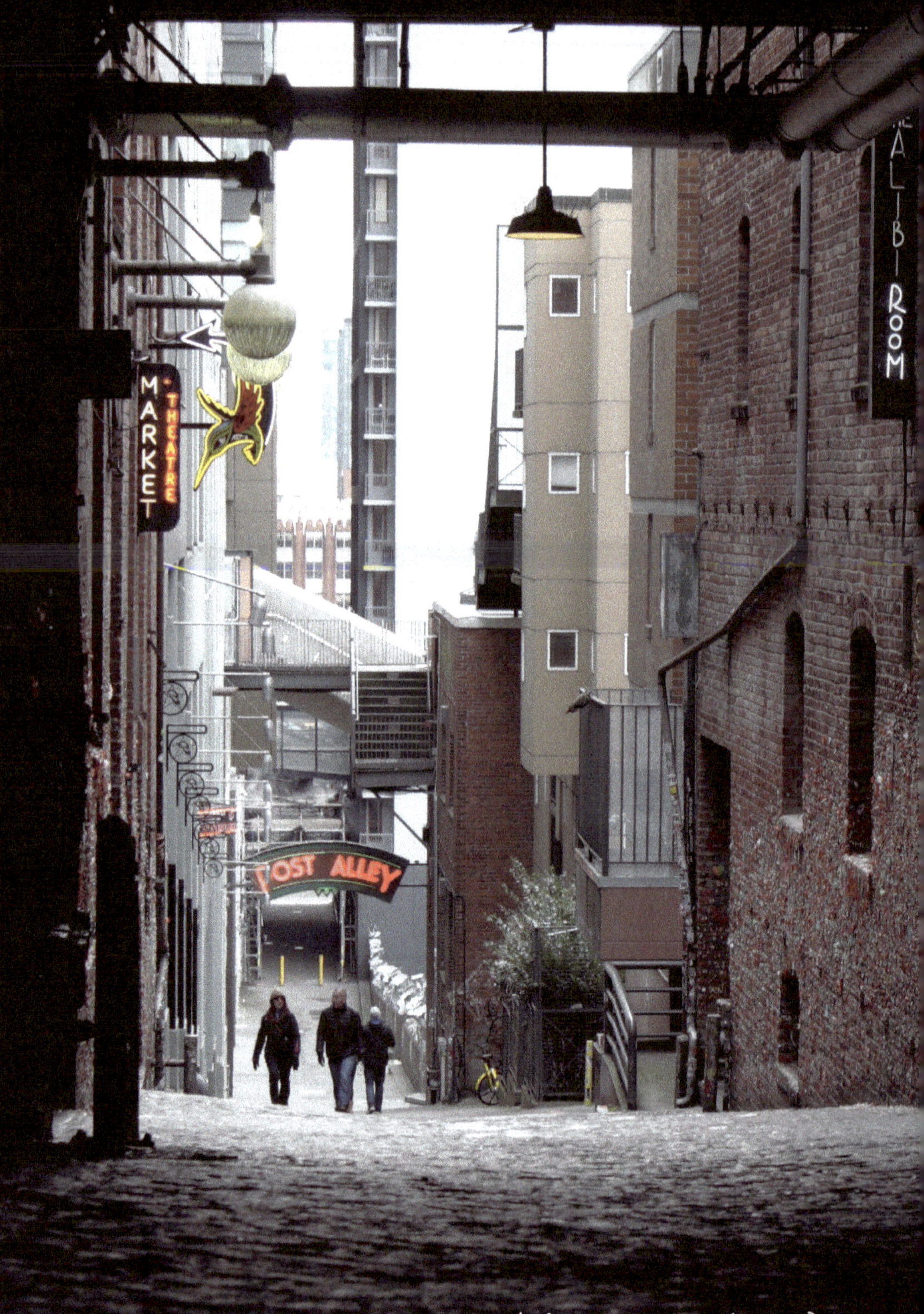
MARKET
THEATRE
OST ALLEY
ALIBI ROOM
Seattle, Washington, USA

Did you know?
To hide the pain
and the history
of people being dragged away
and sold on ships
as slaves
the city swept it all
under the steep streets
that now we walk up
and down
to get to the market
where fish is thrown
and people laugh
as they stick their gum to a wall
that is cleared away
every year

Did you know?
That the resilience of this city
and the way they build
to hide the past
but embrace the present
with their visitors
and the beauty
that this city now brings
to all of those who see
the need to hide
and the need to forget
without that
the city we know
wouldn't exist
with its steep streets
and hidden alleys
and hidden levels
and hidden secrets

Didn't you know?

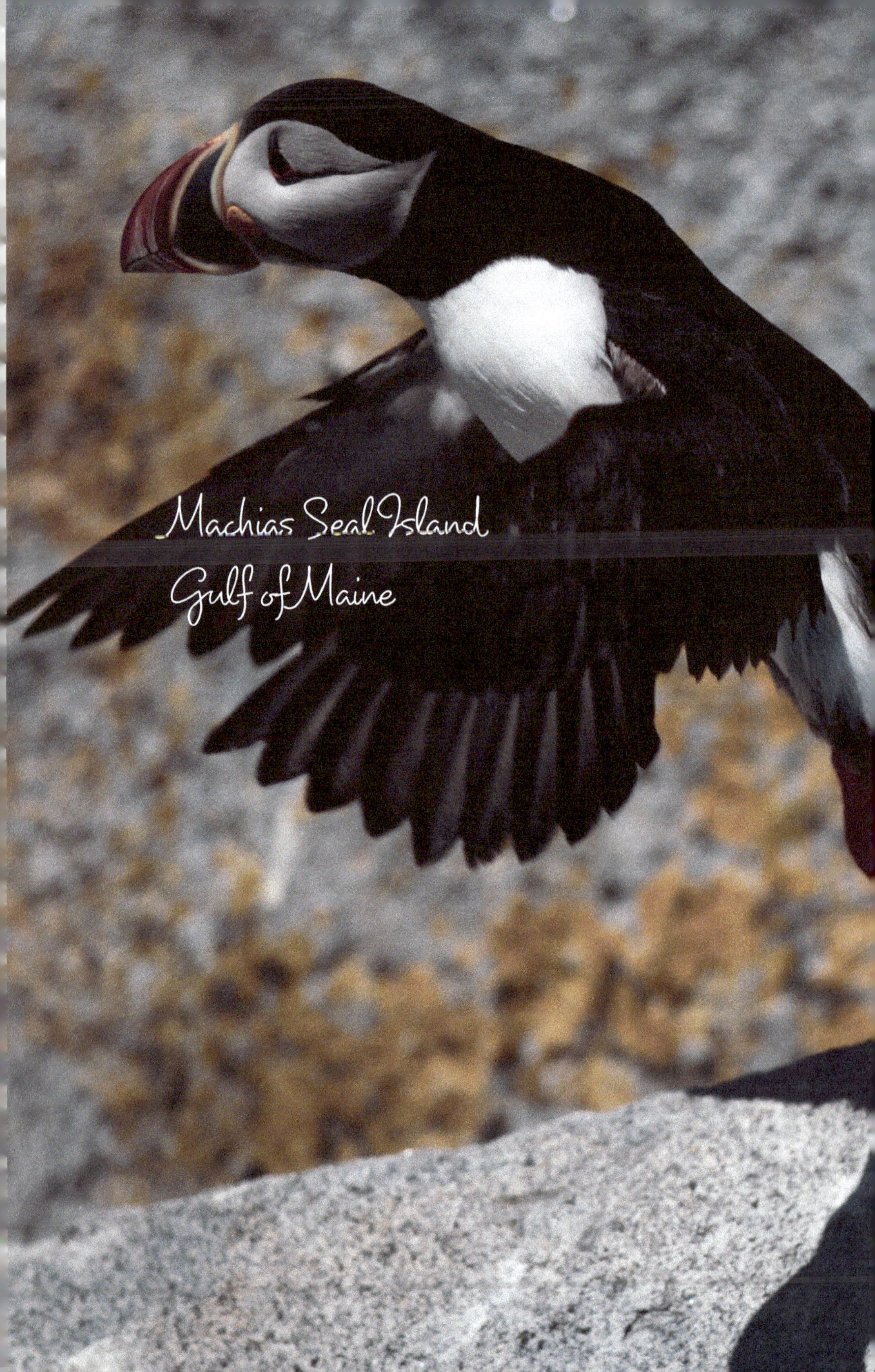
Machias Seal Island
Gulf of Maine

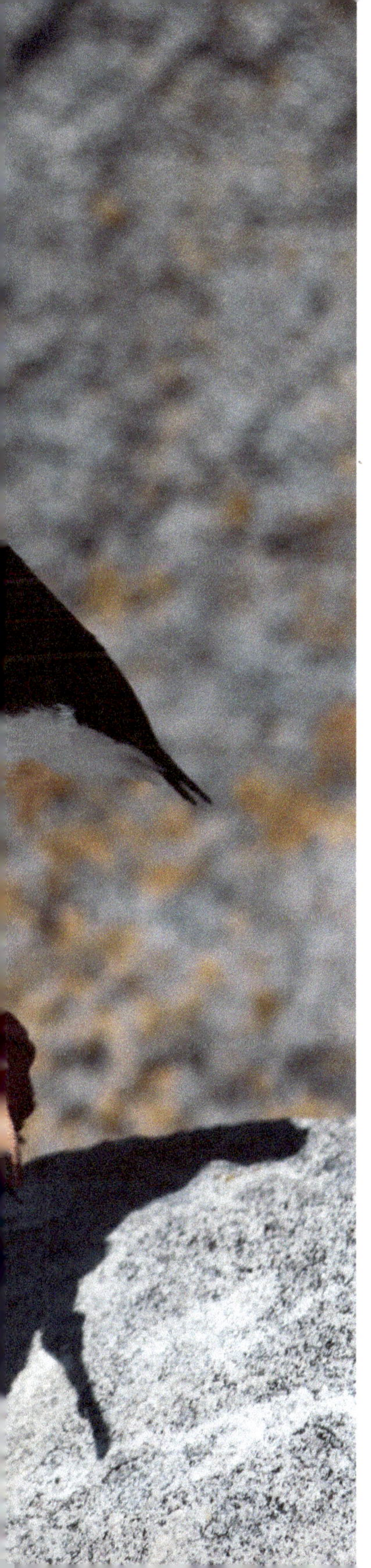

COME INTO FOCUS

Dark inside.
Leaning my head against the wall.
There is a tiny window,
opening to the outside world.
Inside of this dark hut
made from metal slats.
My eyes adjust slowly to the bright blue sky
and between her and me...
there is something else.
Fluttering.
Flapping.
Coming into view.
Orange and black striped beaks
chattering to each other
in a foreign language.
Each black bird
hops and plays
on the grey rocks.
Slide.
Click.
Pop.
Clang.
Noises come from above us
on the metal rafters
as one bird lands,
followed by another.
And another.
As even more
come into focus
out the little window in front.

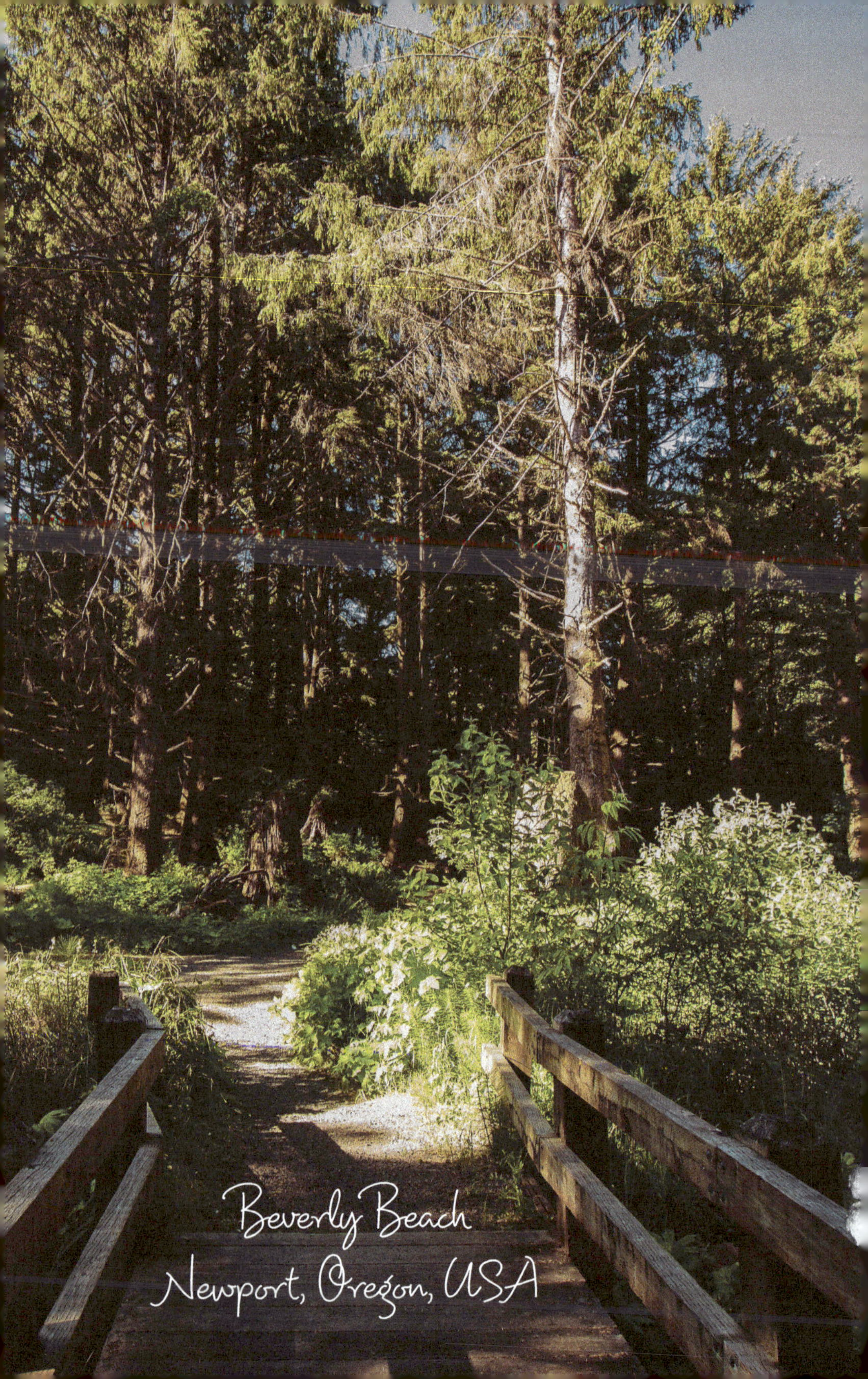
Beverly Beach
Newport, Oregon, USA

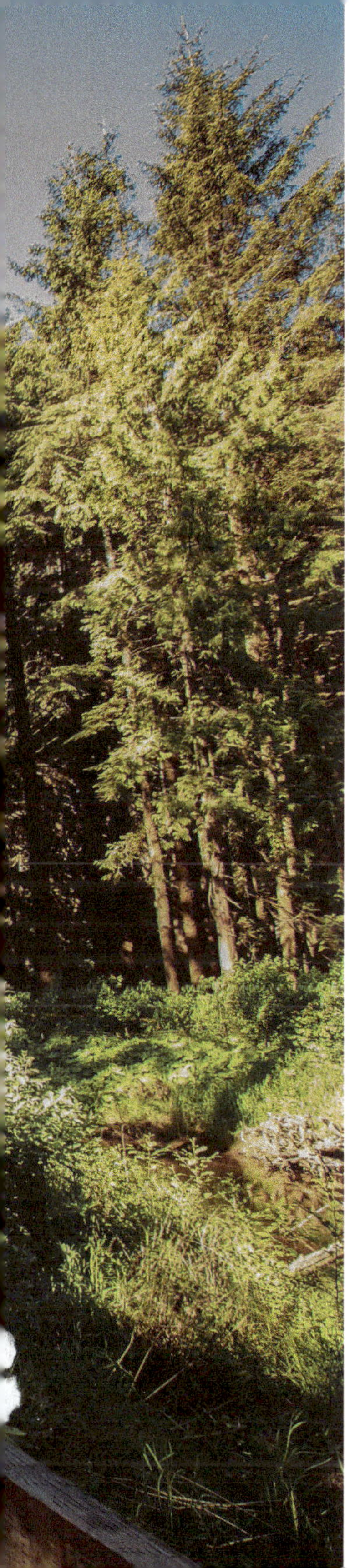

BREATHE DEEP

Breathe deep
in
out
smoke fills my lungs
saturated with the smell of recently cut wood
mingling with flame-licked meat
waiting to be devoured

Breathe deep
in
out
fresh pine fills the air
deep and sharp and fresh and clean
needles falling from the trees above
to coat the ground in green

Breathe deep
in
out
the distant sea spray
thick with salt and bubbling life
as the tide rolls out to reveal the secrets of the ocean
that rumbles just past the trees

Breathe deep
in
out
look up
see the wind blowing past the fragrant pines
carrying stories
of the past
and of the future
as it whistles and sings and blows
and carries the birds home

GROUNDED PLANE

Down and down.
The sweat traces down my back,
in the space between
my pack and the skin.
I watch the people shuffle by.
They forget their phobias
and stand closer
and closer
to others.
Pushing for first place,
where there is no such thing.
Tan lines show
under faces already reabsorbing
the grime of day-to-day life.
Vacation bookended by the travel.
Men in suits shuffling forward,
yelling into headsets
at the people they've left behind.
The air reeks of stale food...
and desperation.
The floors are dirty with crumbs...
and trash
not even seen by the tired eyes
of my peers.

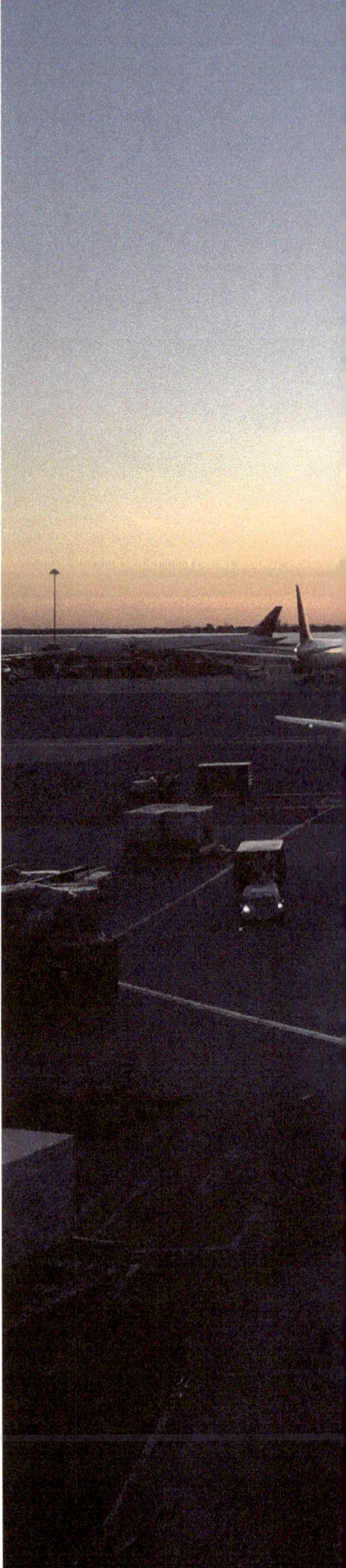

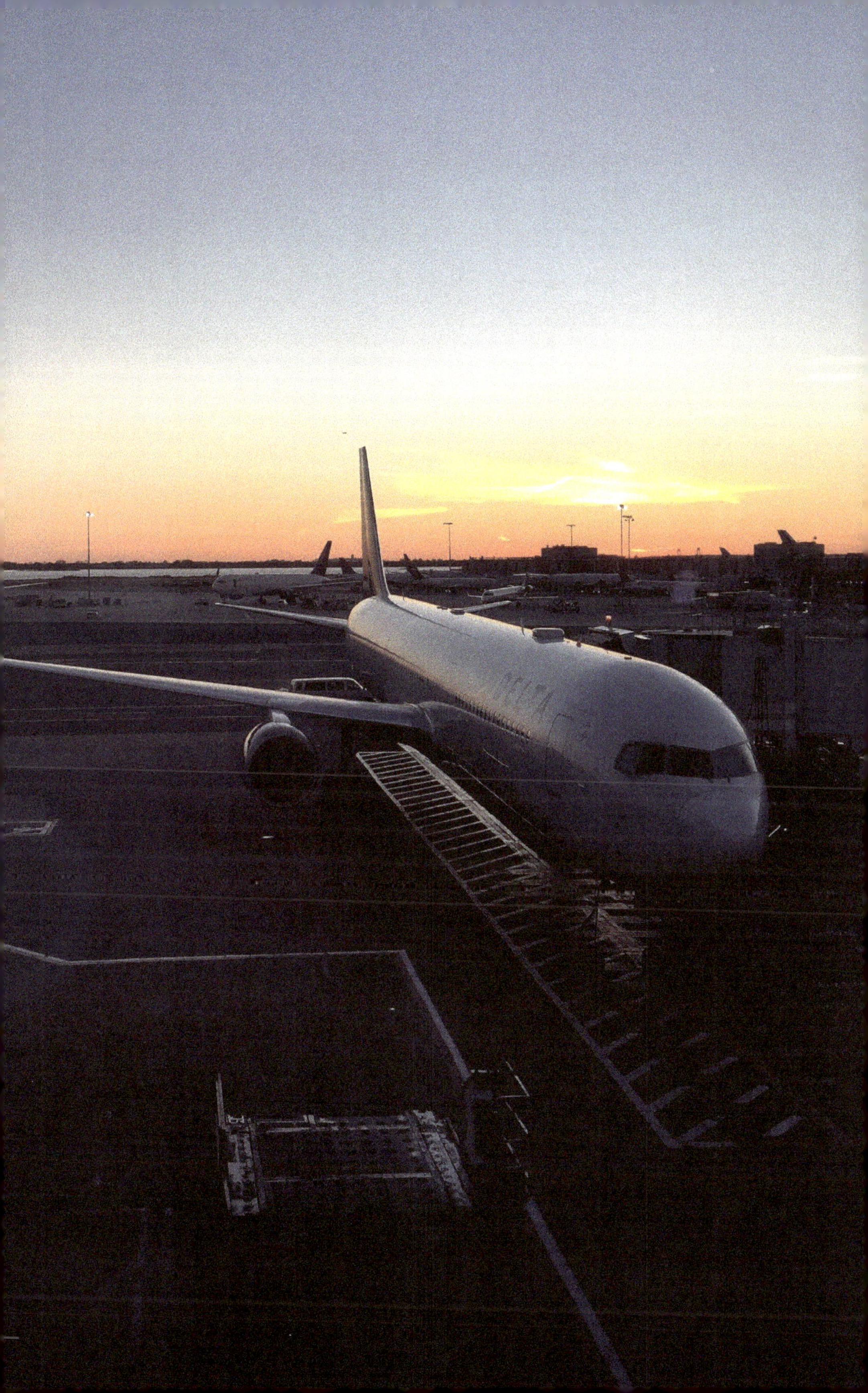

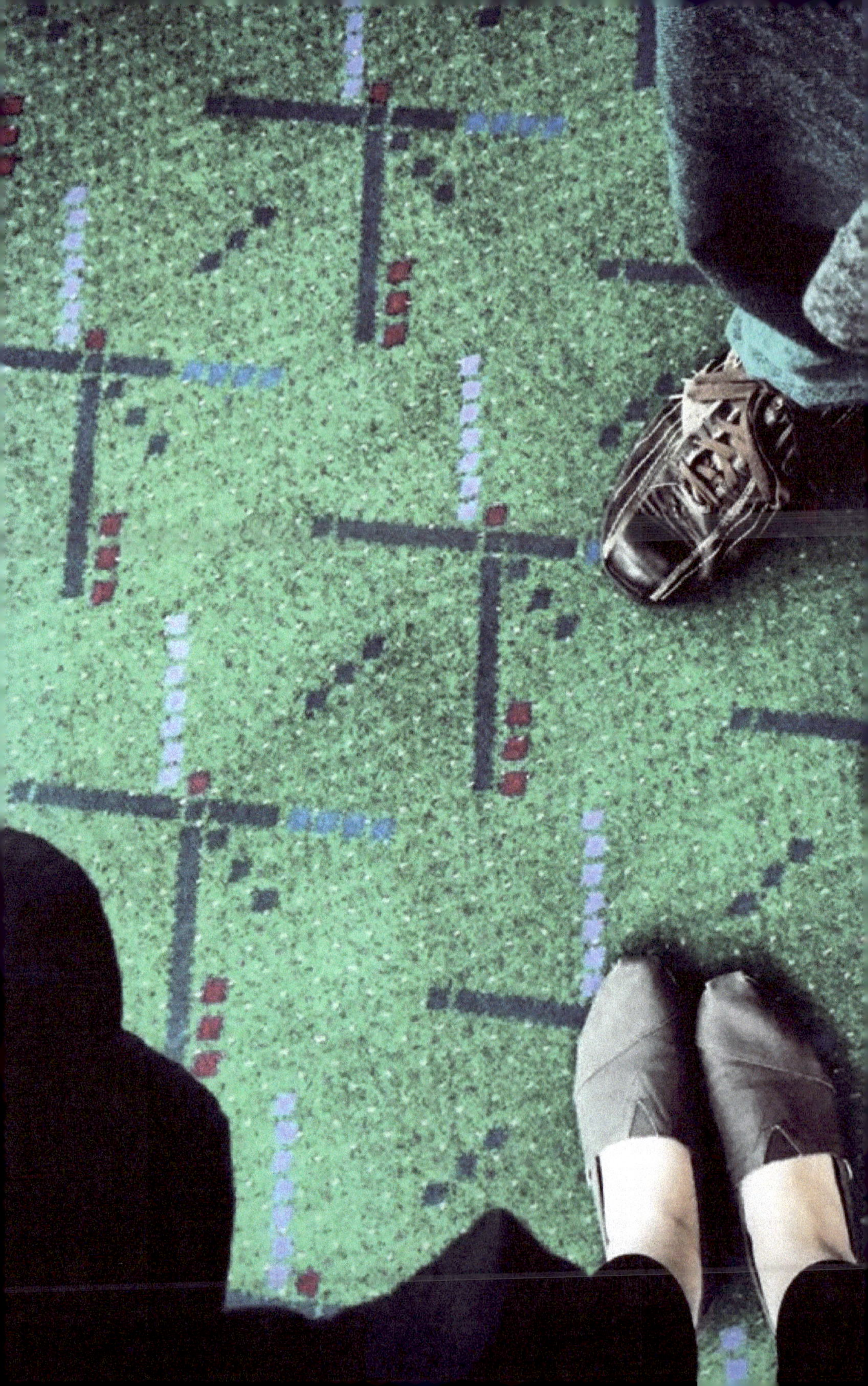

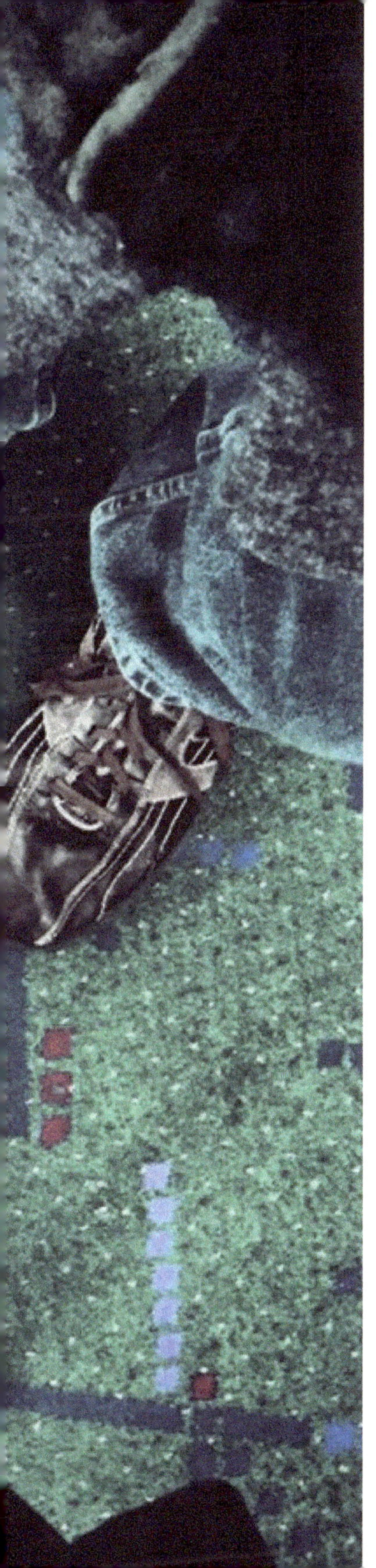

We're each so different,
yet the same,
as we sweat in the stifled
recycled air.
The cheap blue plastic beneath me
squeaks and shifts.
The man, too close to me, coughs.
A child stares longingly out the window
at the blue sky beyond
where the birds fly free,
but man is compressed.
Crammed.
Prodded.
Pinched.
I follow his eyes towards the freedom.
A baby screams.
A foot kicks my bag.
More trash.
More noise.
All the same.
We are all the same.
I want to scream like the baby
who is still at full volume.
How will I ever make it?
How will I survive?
As I near hour six… of my flight delay.

COOL BROWN BEER

The cold brown liquid
slips down my throat.
The brown of the beer matches
the brown of the wood paneling.
Shiny and smooth,
small chips and bubbles running through.
Soft music of my teenage years
playing over the distant speakers.
The supple leather of the seat
cushions my ass as I sit.
A man rambles in Gaelic at the bar top.
The bartender watches it all.
Much older than those he waits on.
Has been here for so long.
Years of his life.
He's seen more than what sits here tonight.
My eyes move back to the glass in my hand
and I take a drink of the cool brown beer
in the relaxed brown bar
that sits at the corner of
a brown brick street
and realize
there is no one here but me.

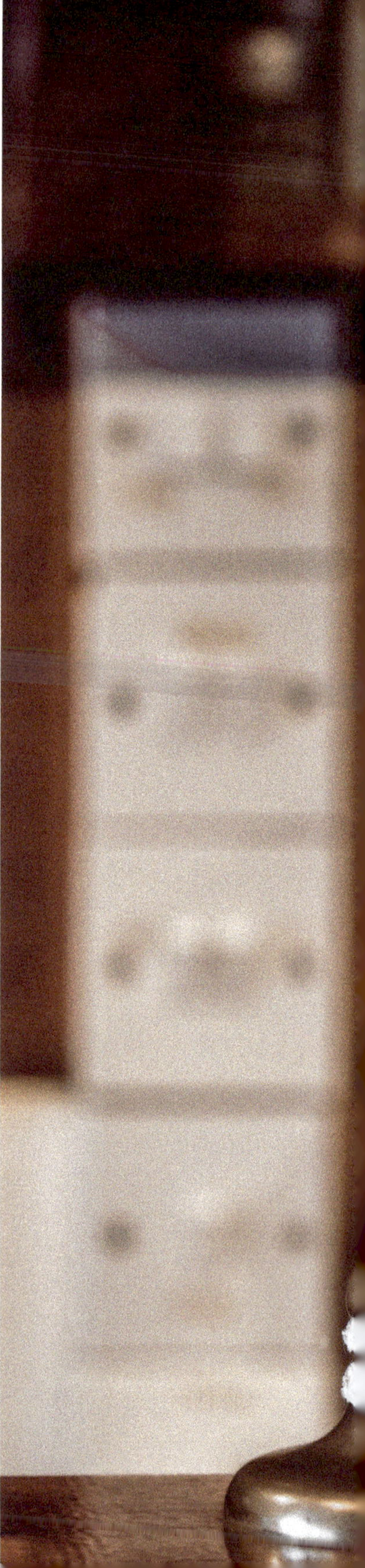

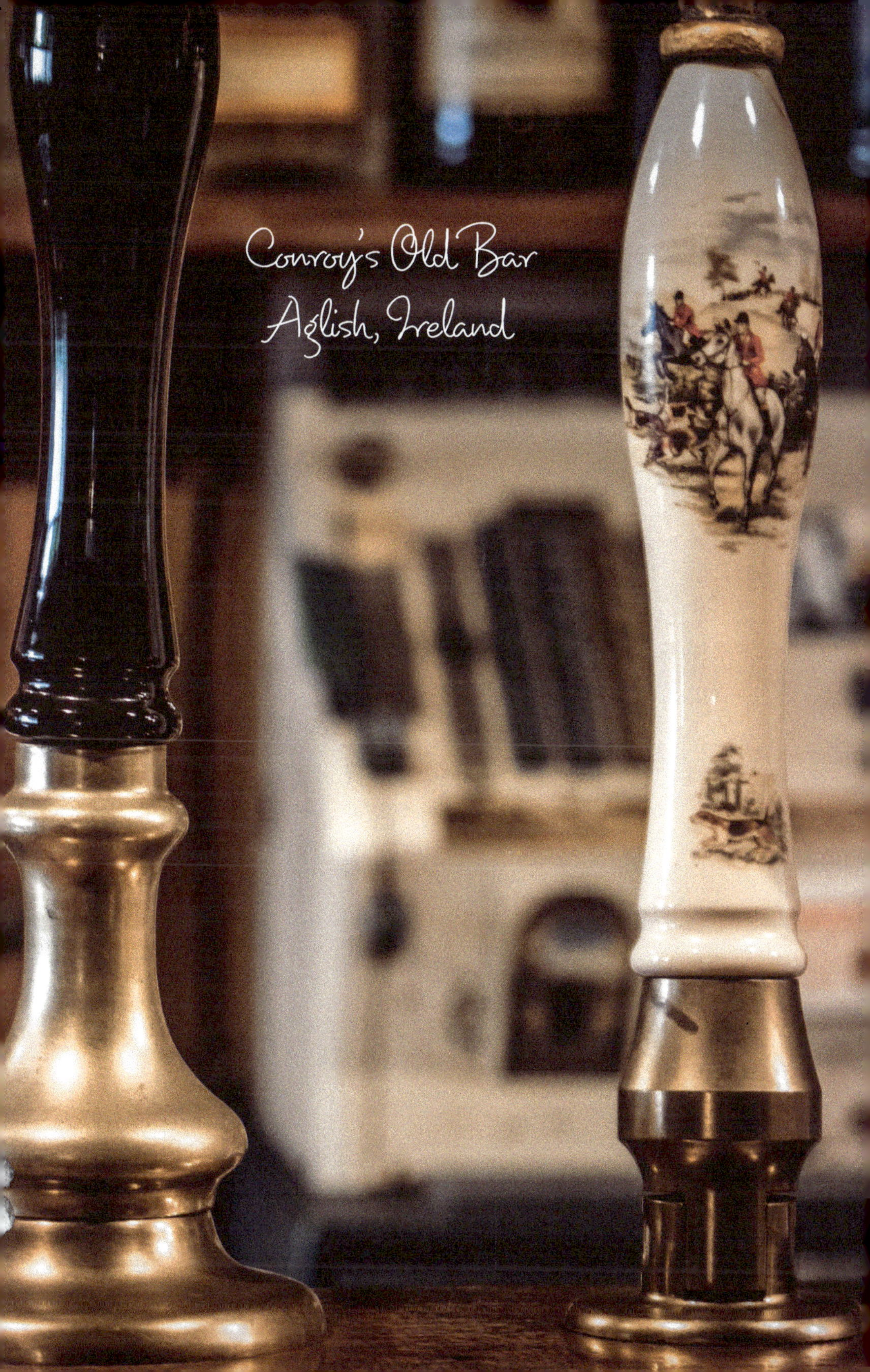
Conroy's Old Bar
Aglish, Ireland

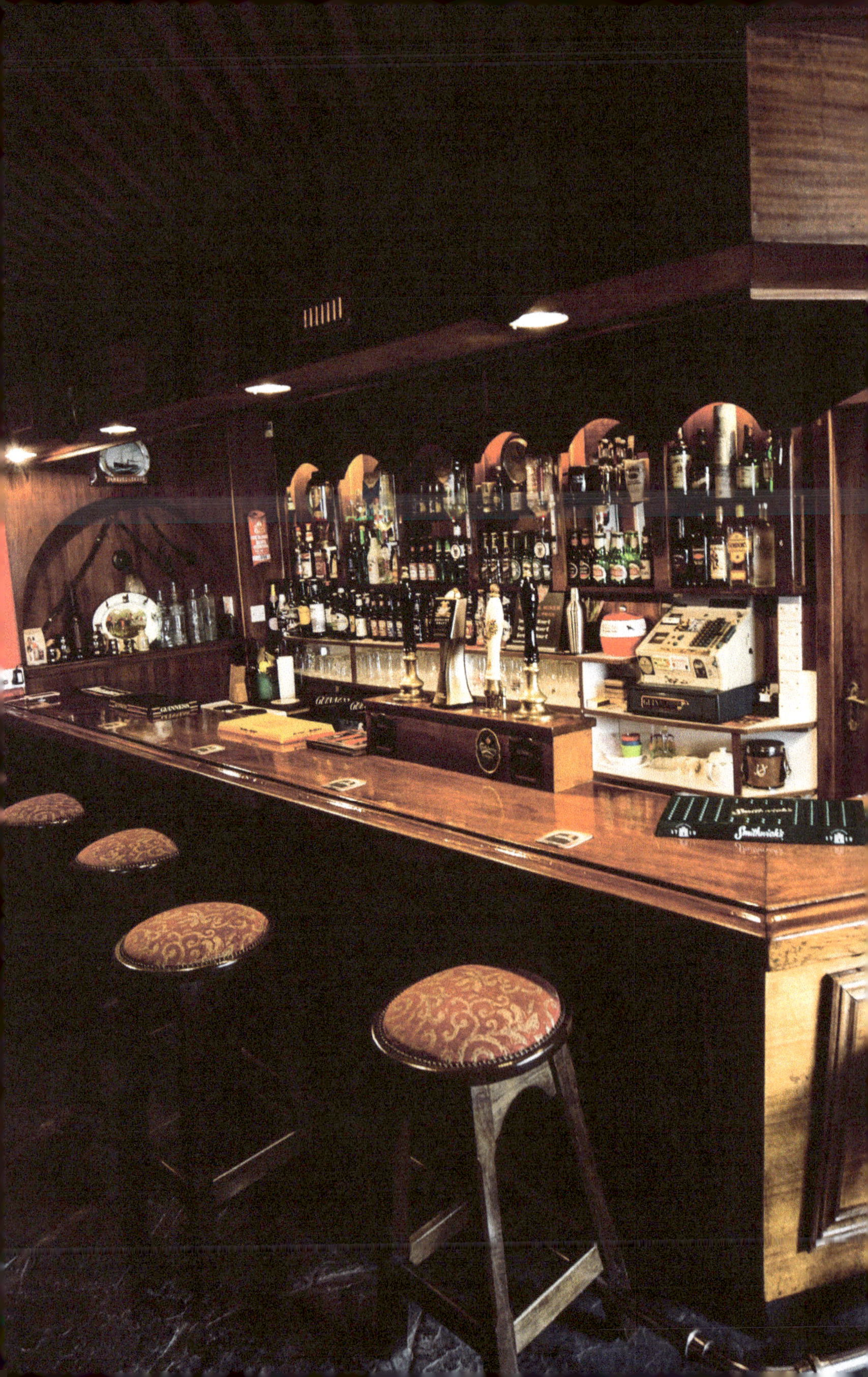
GUINNESS
Smithwick's

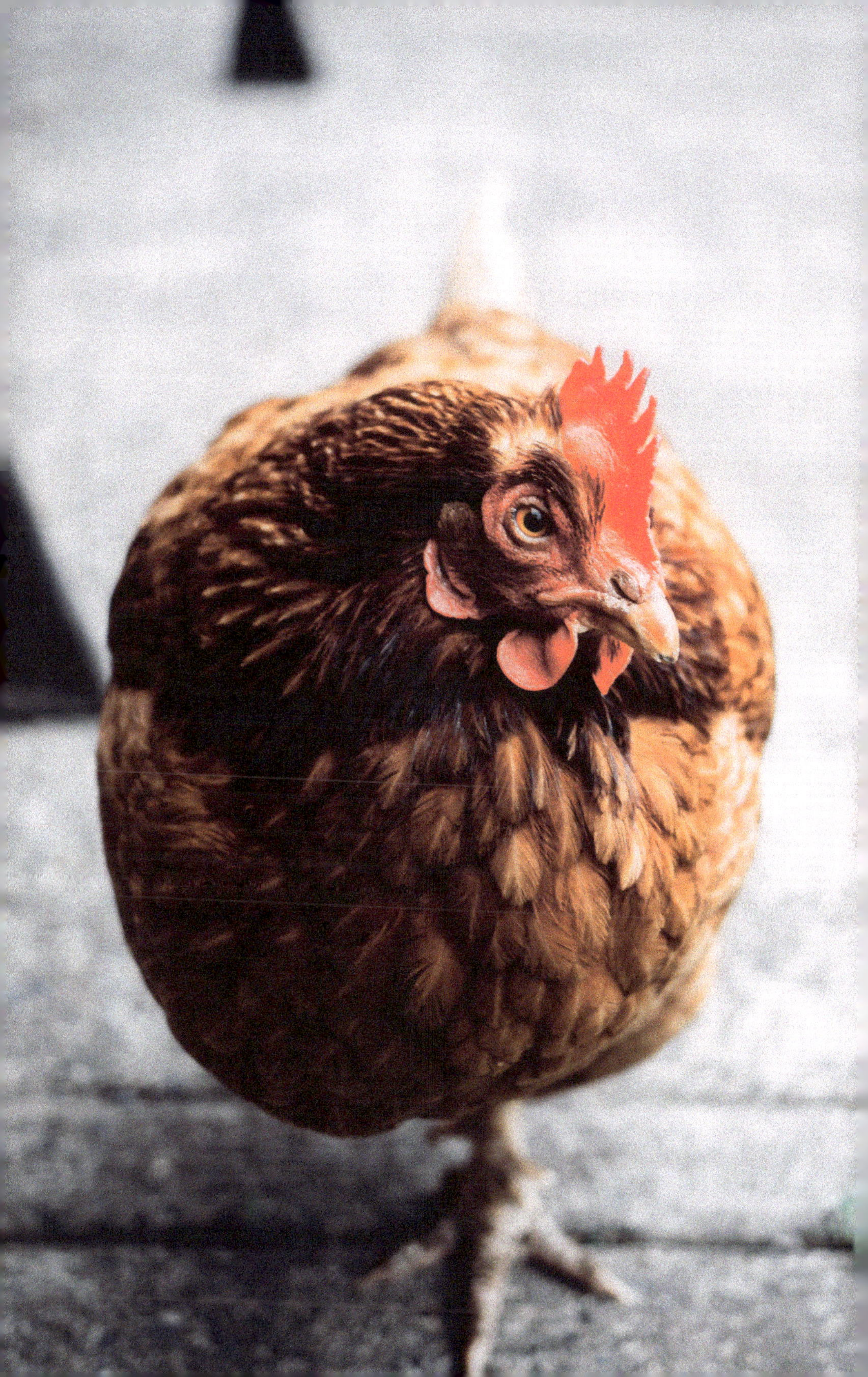

REFLECTION

The red lights reflect
against the still waters below.
Senses muddled
from the beer
and the brownie.
Both shared
in places loud and filled
with poetry and laughter
in languages from the world.
The air smells of hops and grass
and faintly of sweat.
In this place filled with beauty
of stone and flesh.
History of fishermen...
craftsmen...
tradesmen...
Now their footsteps followed
By the businessmen...
accountants...
travelers...

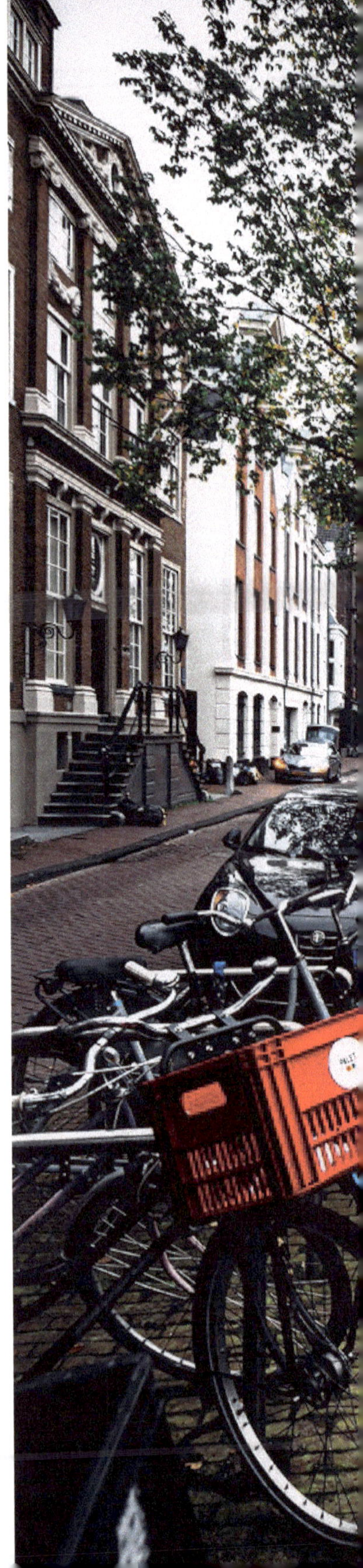

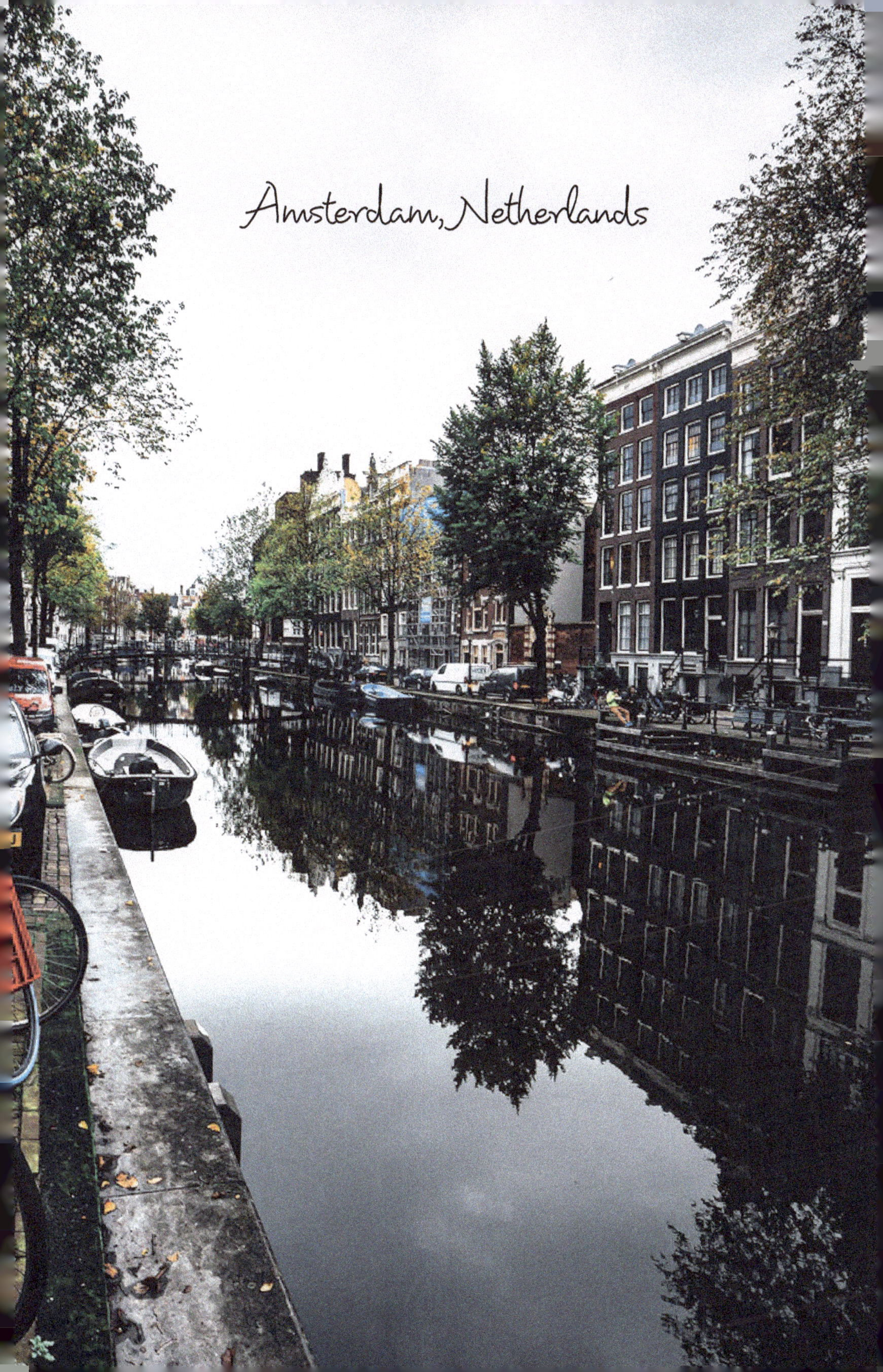
Amsterdam, Netherlands

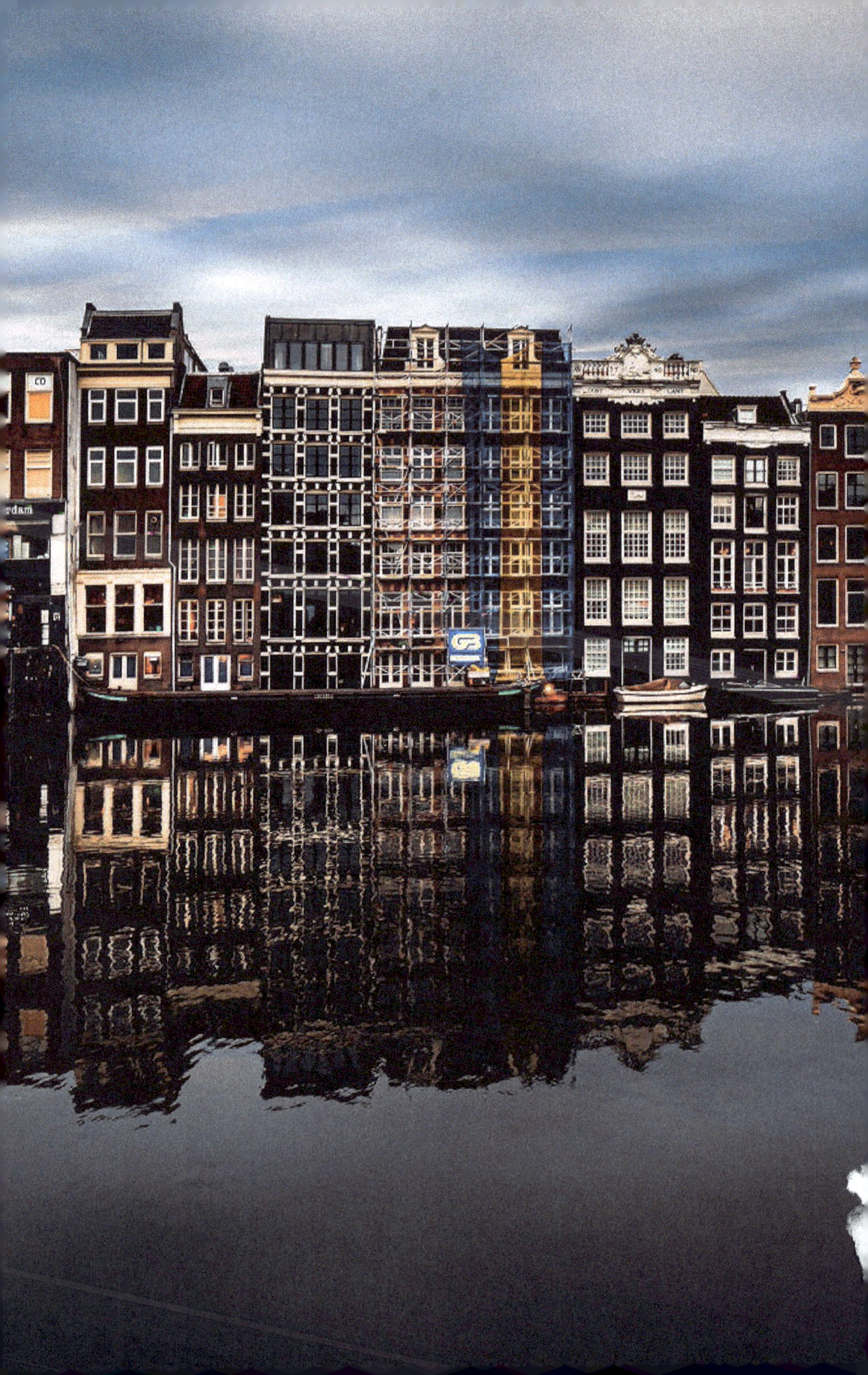

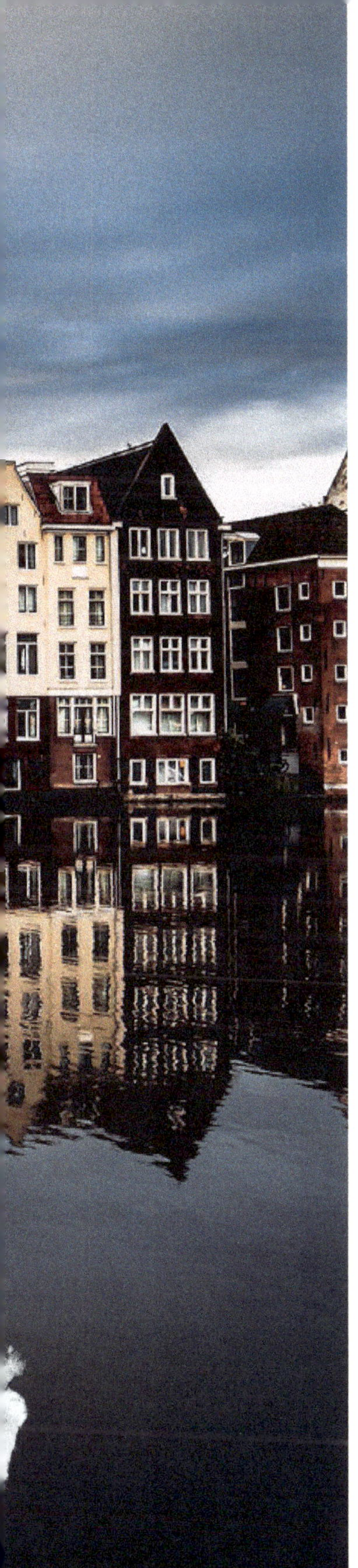

The night transforms the canals,
filled with cobblestone history
and written inspiration.
Now to pulsating music
and the wave of a slender hand.
People walk in groups
past other groups.
Laughing and stumbling.
All watching in the same direction.
As others watch them
from the shadows.
Waiting for a lowered guard,
allowing for a swift hand.
Lifting a wallet...
or two.
In a place filled with mesmerizing awe
both day and night.
A man looks around
before walking out of a secret door
and into the night.
Behind him
a light turns back on
and joins the others
as the red lights reflect
against the still waters below.

TO NAMCHEE

legs burning
lungs too
each step harder than the last
my breath bellows in front
of my face
as I sigh out
and lift my heavy boot to the next
giant rock
and push
slowly
step up
breathe in
break
the sound of bells in the distance
warning of the donkeys on their way
quicker than us
packs heavier than ours
as their bells chime with each step
the snow falls
the wind blows
we climb further
step
step
break
is there no end
as we go...

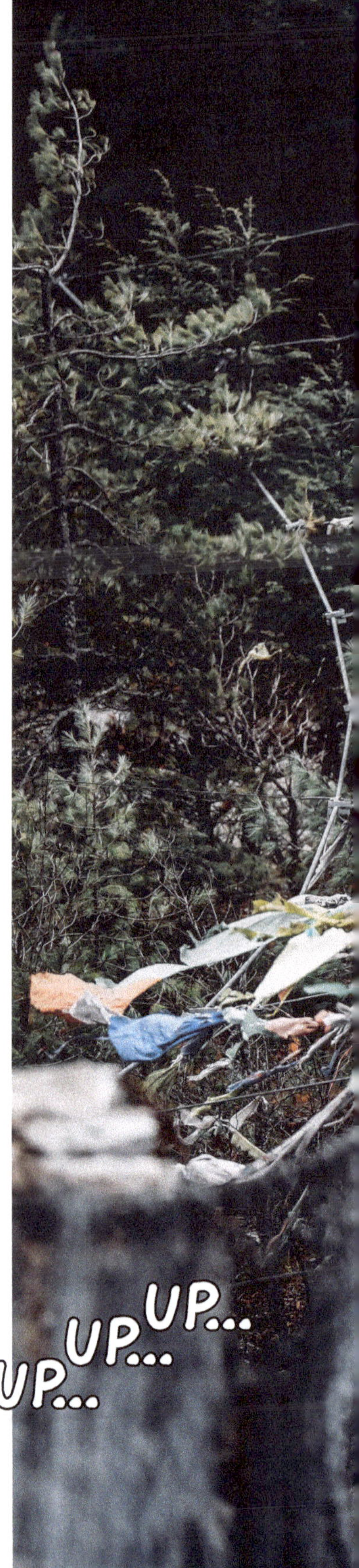

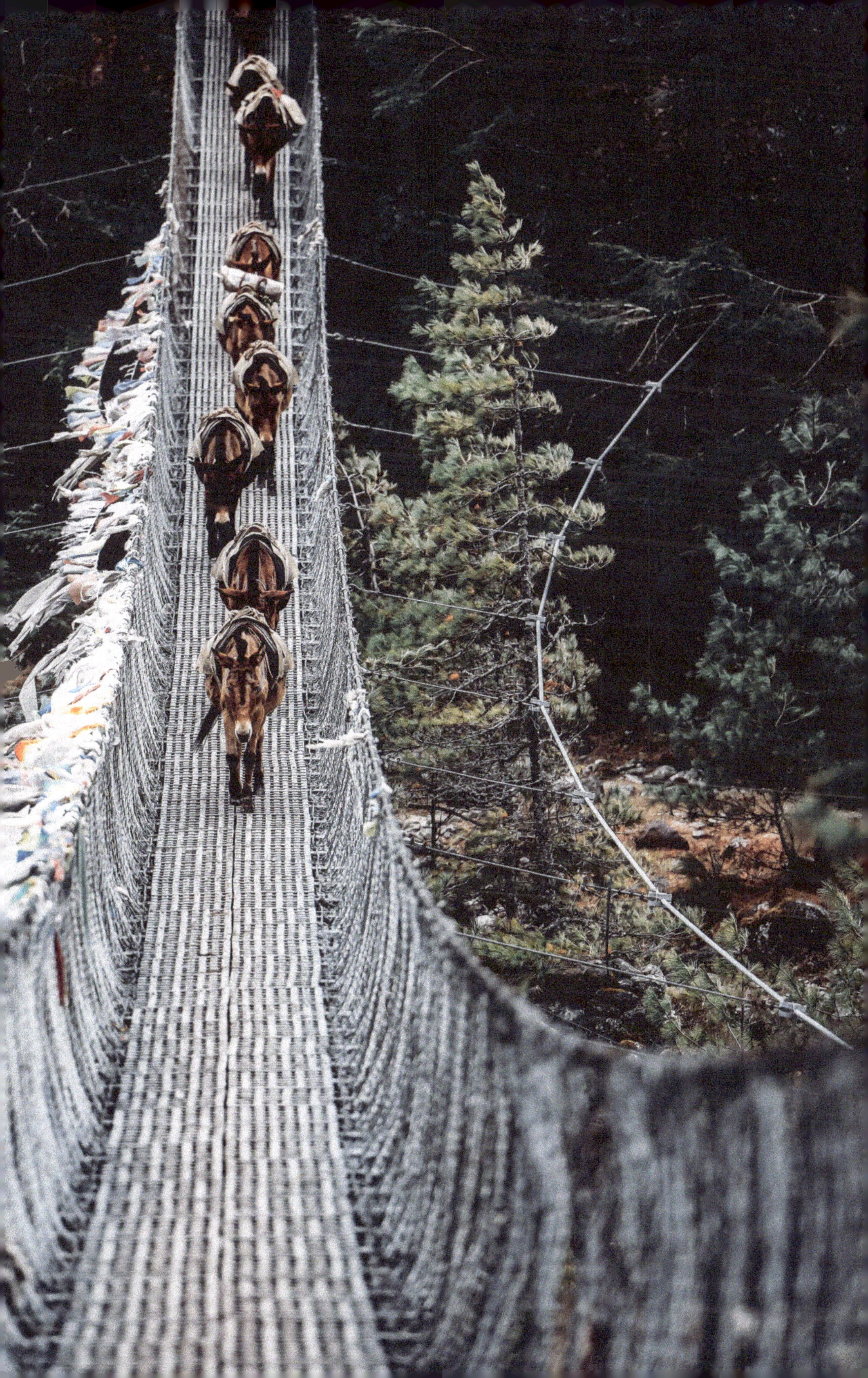

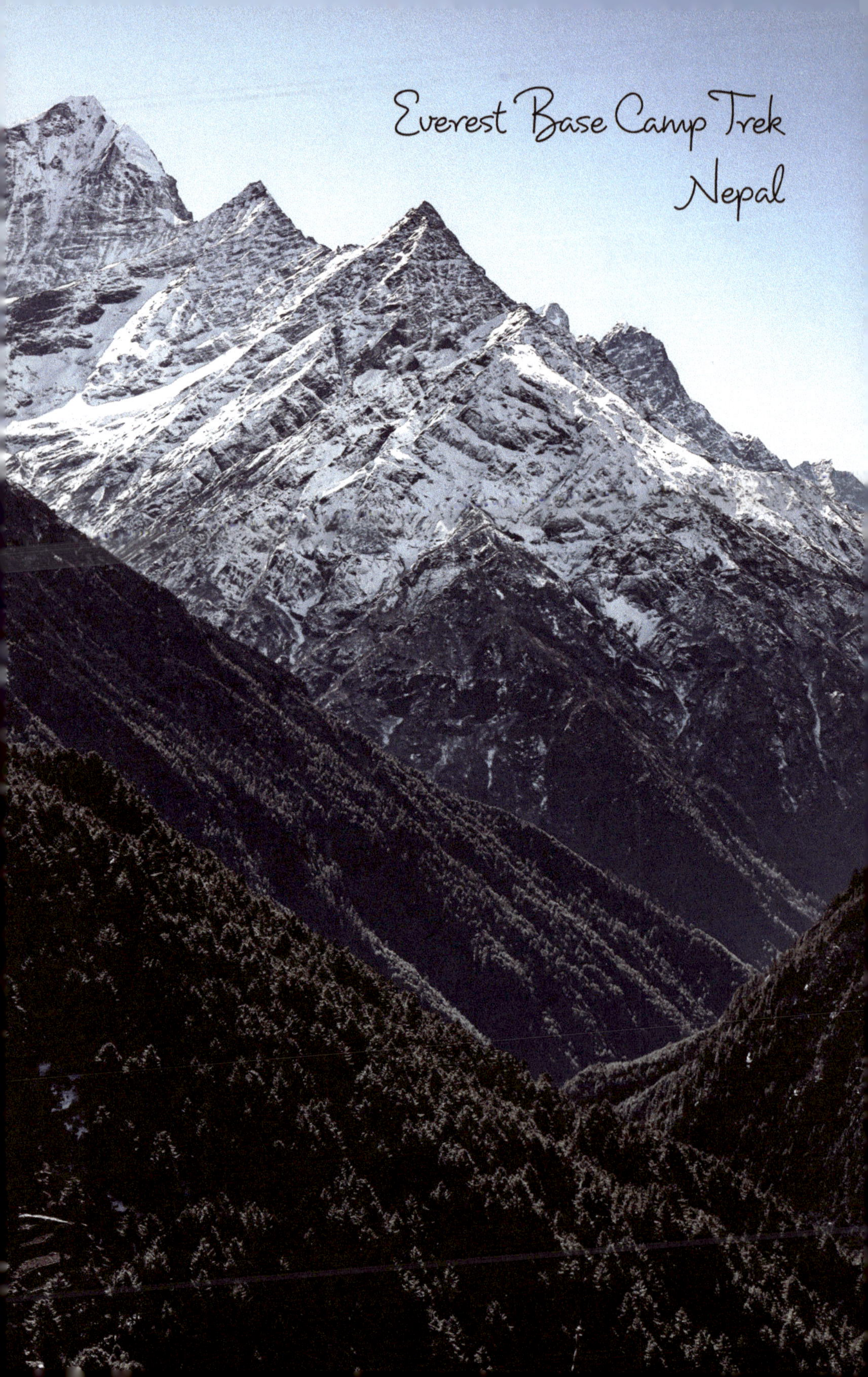
Everest Base Camp Trek
Nepal

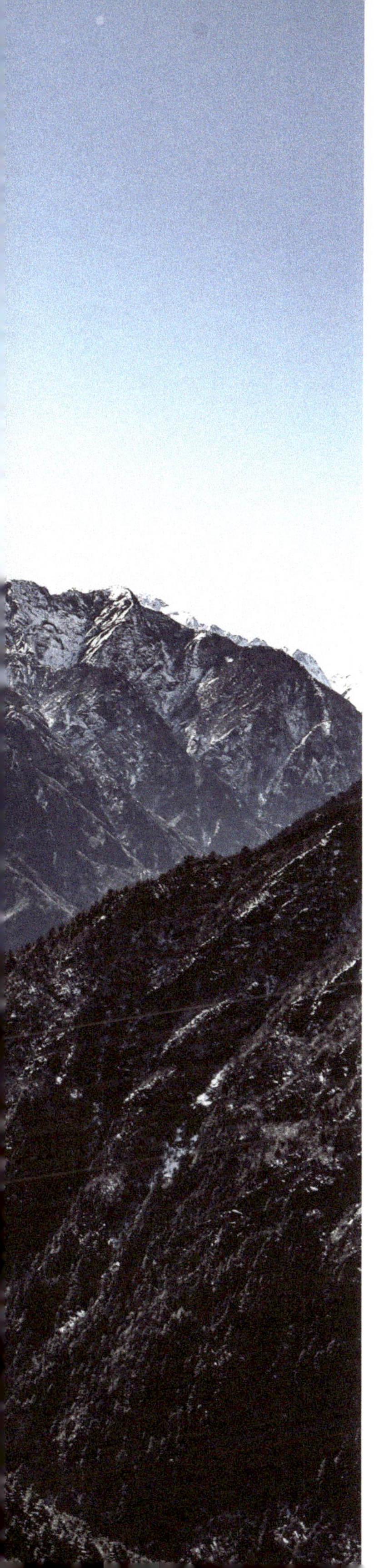

the snow blinds us and
wets our gloves
and we keep going
step
step
break
breathe
the snow stops as
the sky opens to show bright blue
revealing mountains reaching
for the sky
harsh black rock
climbing up
up
up
cut off by the white peaks
sun warms us as we turn towards
the bright city sitting
in the rock placed
where it does not belong
yet where it was always meant to be
the heaviness leaves my lungs
and my legs
as I set my eyes on the
beauty
of Namchee

WE WILL SUSTAIN

Do I make a sound
if you aren't there to hear it,
when I fall or get taken down?
Is there a thud
when I slam against the ground?

I've been here for years,
me and my brothers.
Through the pain and the fears,
we've stood here and lasted
and will remain with our tears.

We provide families shade
and a moment's break
as they drive through the glade.
Standing tall and proud.
People took what we gave.

You leave your trash
hunkered in our needles.
Take selfies unabashed
against our trunks
next to the initials you slashed.

The silence is golden,
better than the sounds of a screen.
Us trees, so thickly woven.
Think of us and our future
the next time you feel so emboldened.

We will sustain
against all odds
as mother nature maintains.
You love us and we you,
so here we'll remain.

Just please remember us
as you teach your young ones
to try not to make a fuss.
Letting others build and pollute.
Now it's time to adjust.

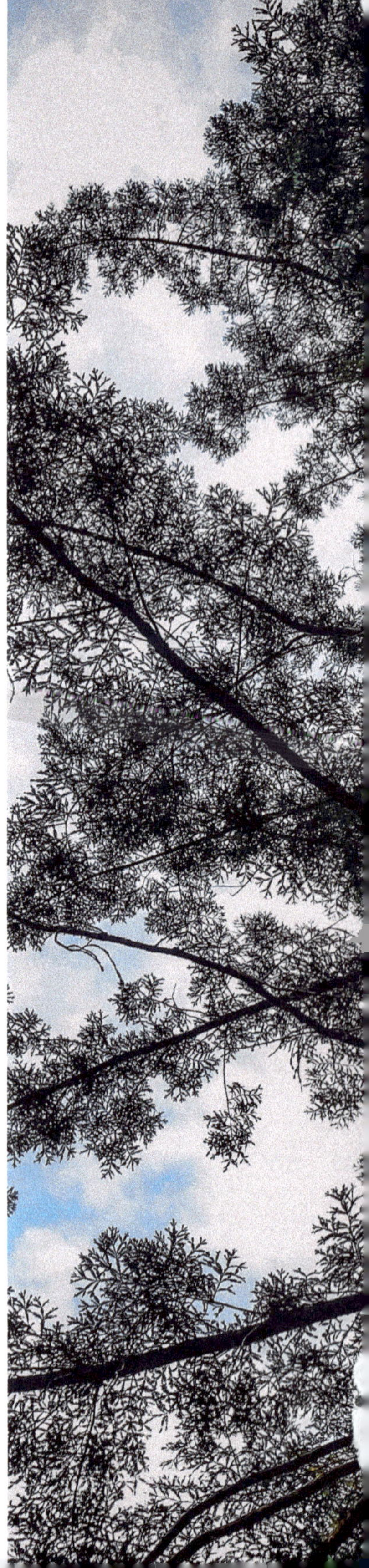

The Redwoods - California, USA

LET'S CALL HER MARY

There is laughter now
as a boy jumps
out from behind a tree.
His friends snickering,
pretending they didn't just jump
in fear.
Two women walking past,
gossiping
and giggling.
A child clings to the head of his father
as he sits upon his shoulders.
Eyes bright,
watching it all.
But there…
beneath the sounds
of present day life
and feet skipping by.
A whisper.
A cry.
Carried from the past,
hidden in the tree.
A plea.
"Please save me."
Lean in closer.
Squeeze your eyes shut.
Drown out the other sounds.
The whisper grows louder.
What else does the tree say?
Louder still…

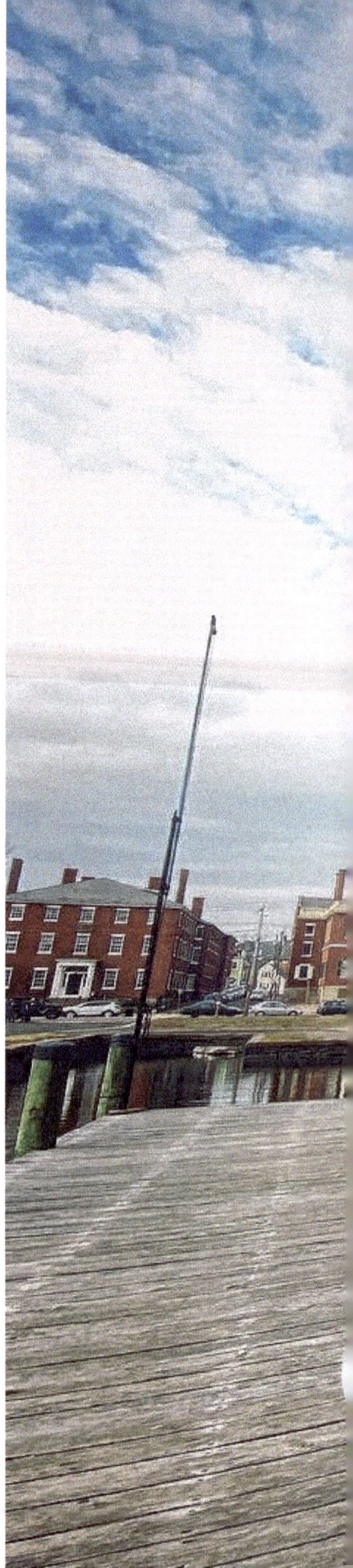

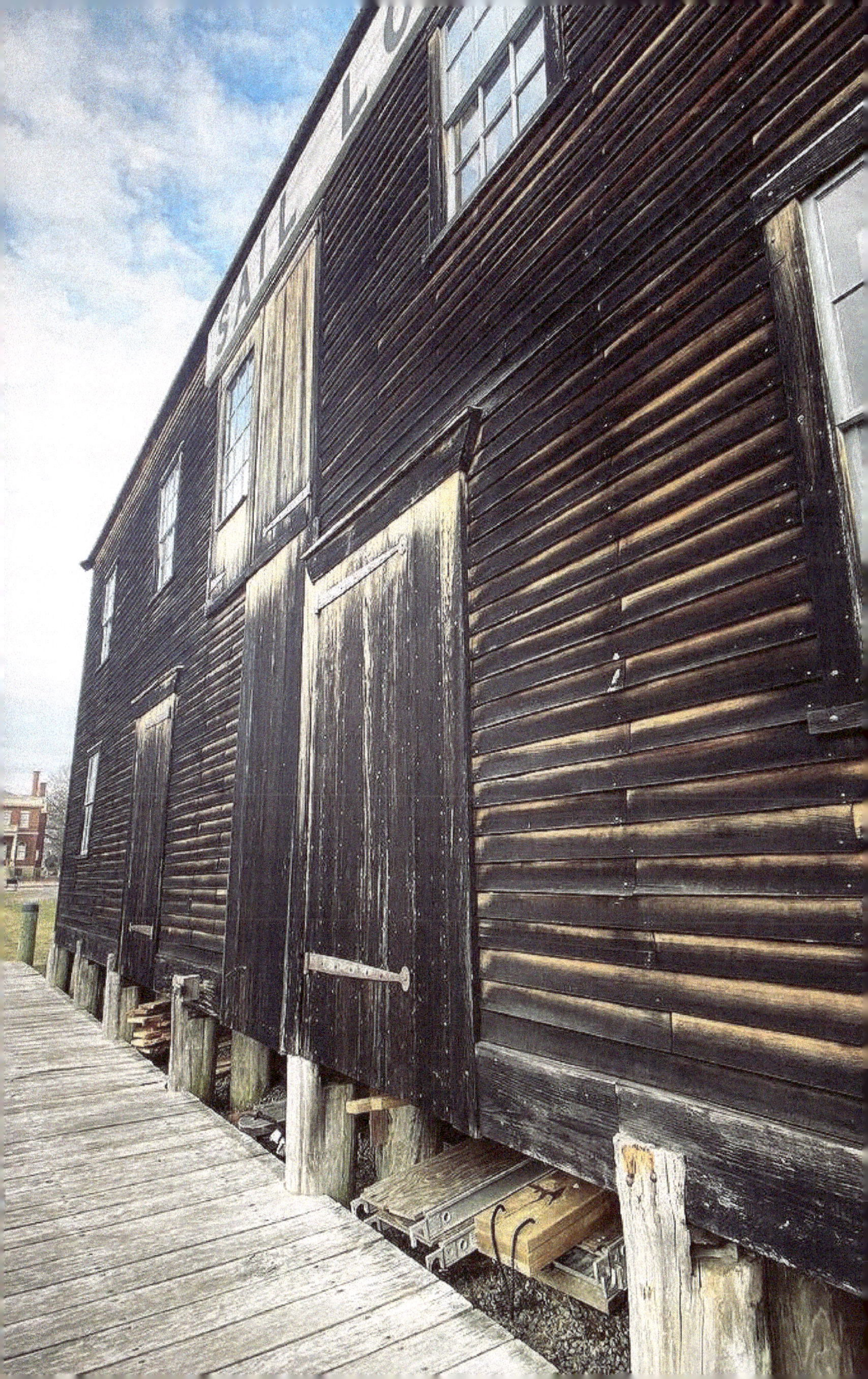
SAIL

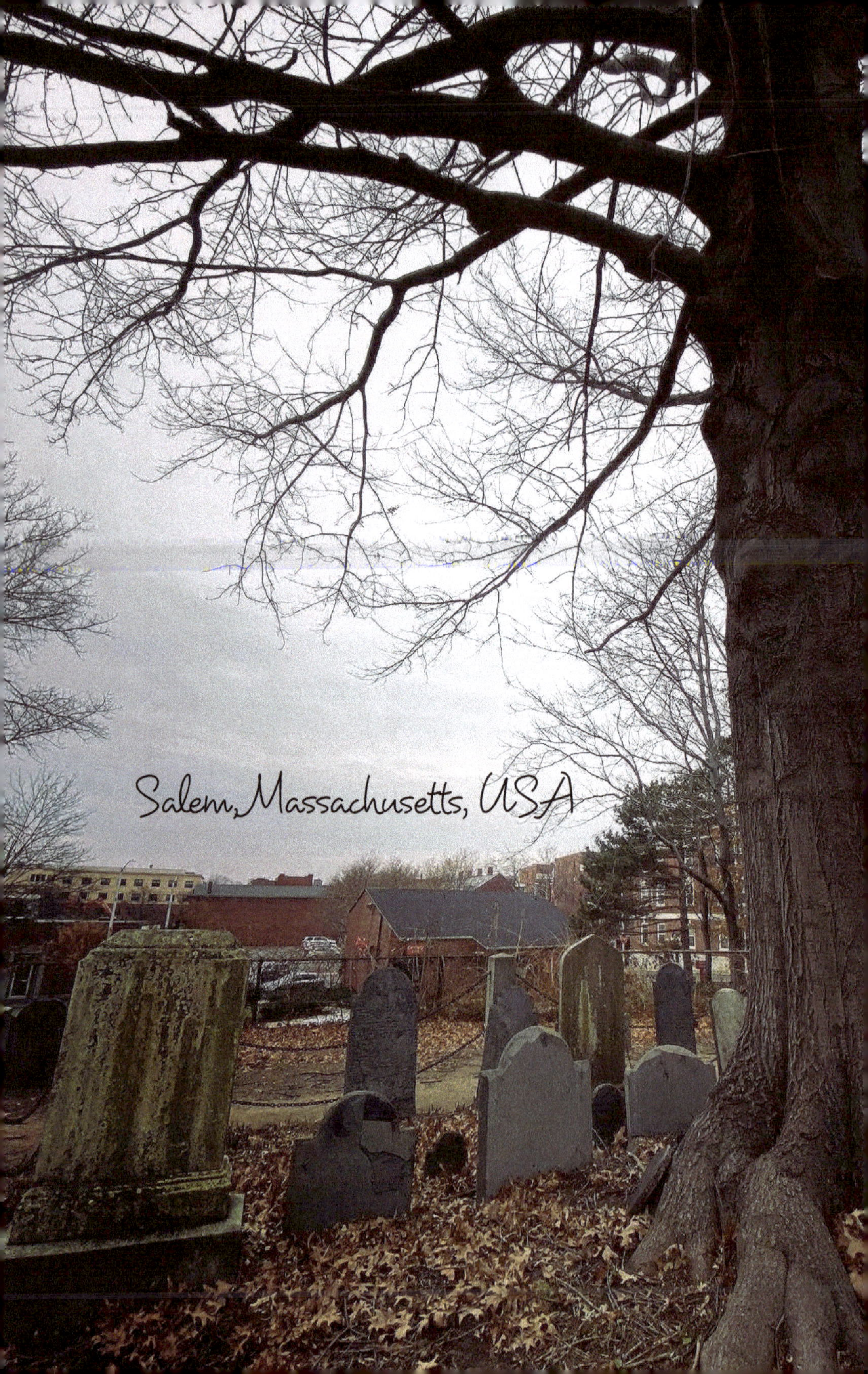
Salem, Massachusetts, USA

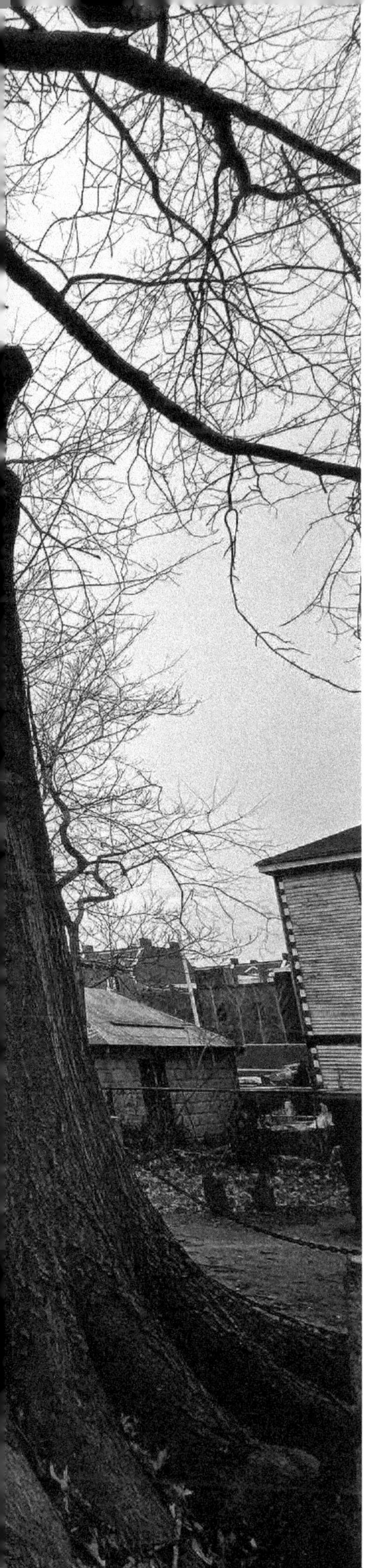

"There was a girl
Let's call her Mary
She needed attention
They should have been wary

She pointed her finger
And loudly screamed
She was afflicted
Or so it would seem

There was a man
Let's call him John
He would shout to hang them all
Until they were all gone

Witch, Witch
The fearful people shouted
Their ignorance took over
More "witches" were outed

"I'm innocent!"
An old woman cries
Right before the rope pulled tight
And the light leaves her eyes"

Jump back from the tree.
Eyes open wide.
The secrets the tree shared,
they're hard to hear.
But you know...
Or you hope...
People are no longer
driven by fear,
or ignorance,
or listen blindly to
an unknowable foe...
Right?
The sounds of life return
to full volume.
The secrets of the tree
slipping away.
Gaze following the tree up
past a carving of **H+A**
Stop at the branch
and the faint ghost of swaying feet.
The image getting lighter
as it fades
away.

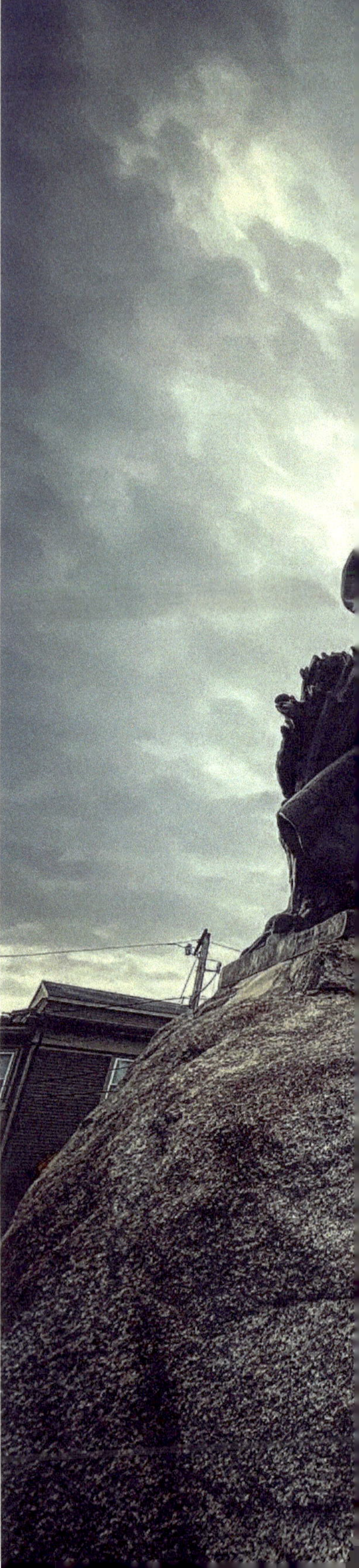

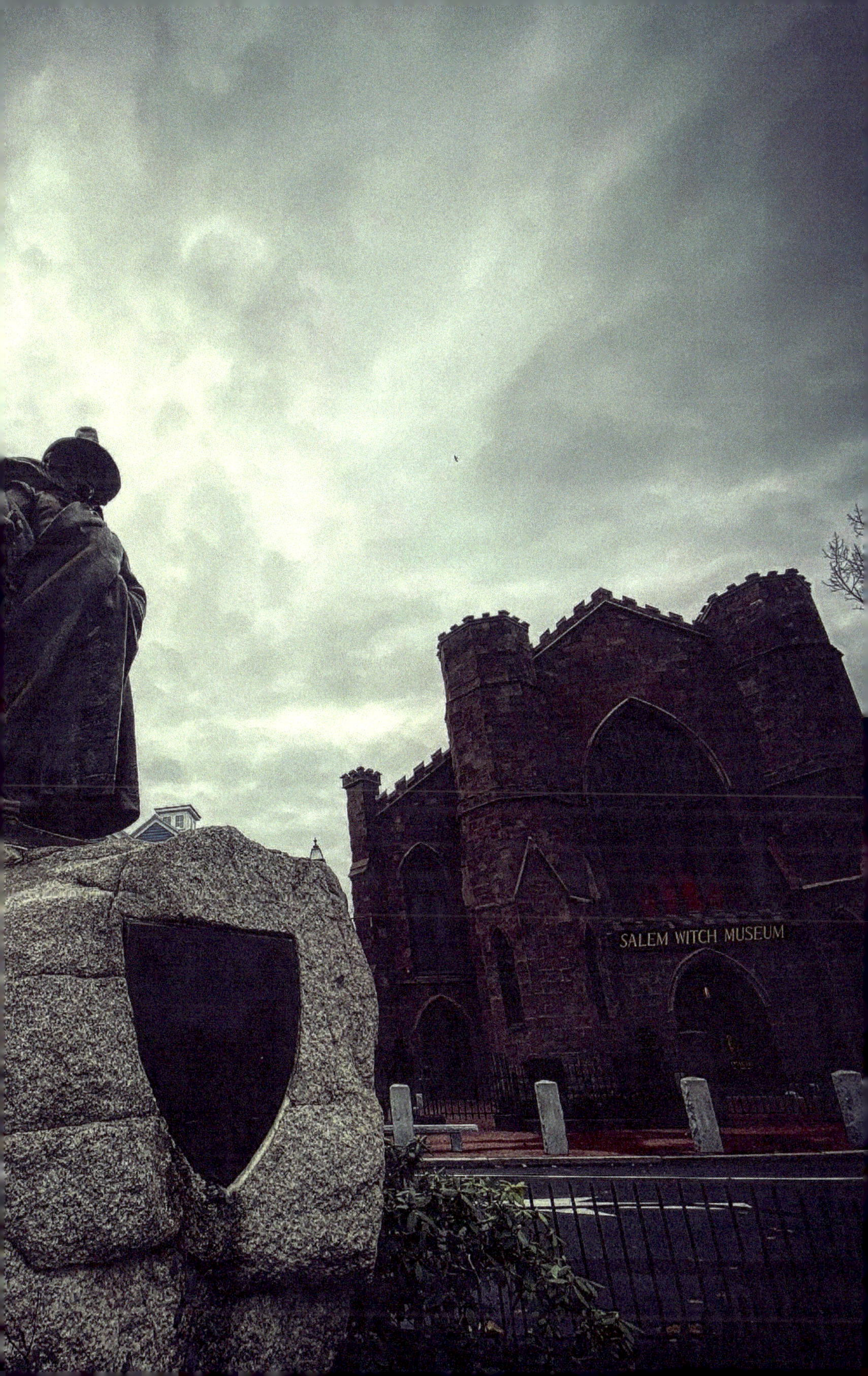
SALEM WITCH MUSEUM

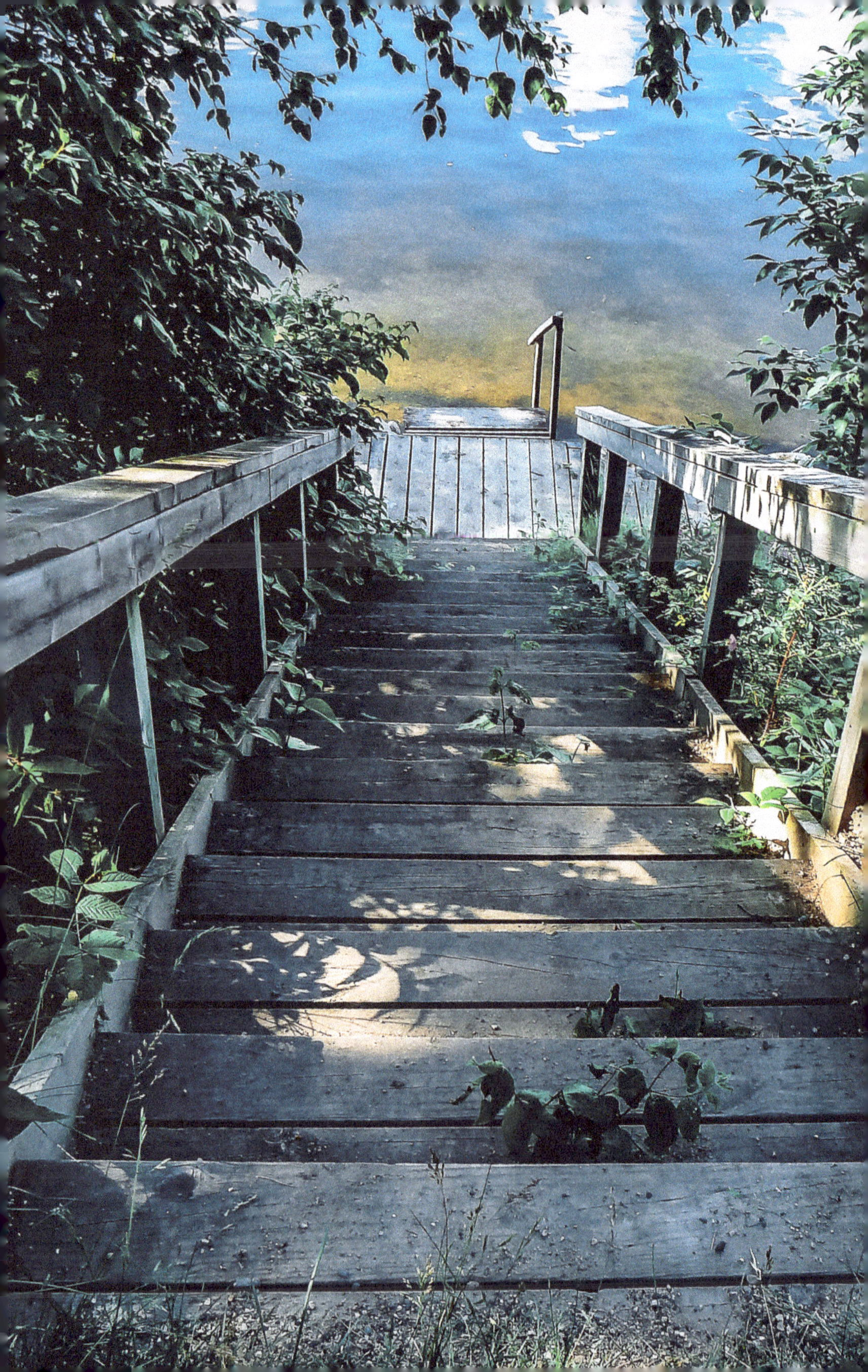

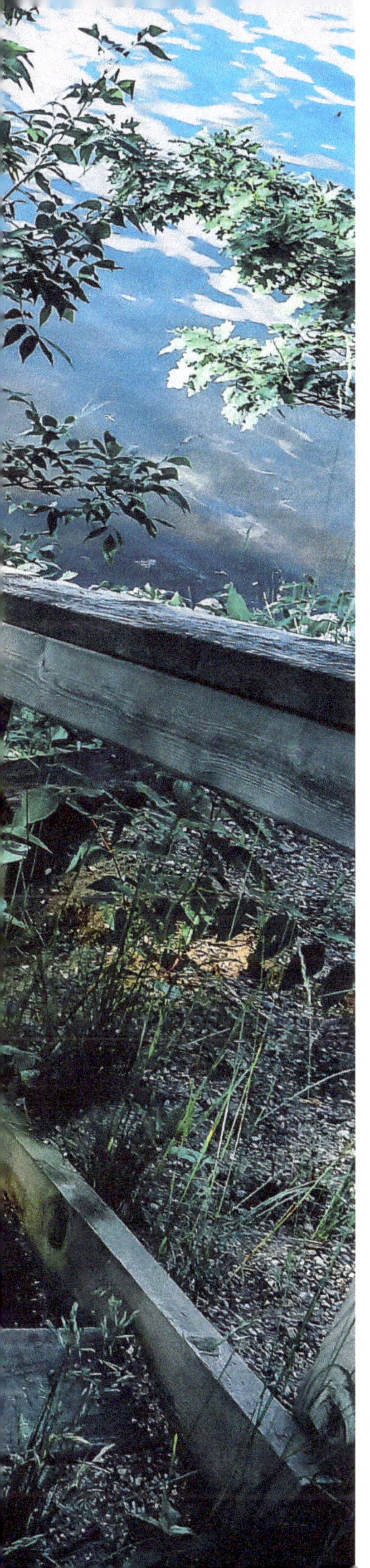

ONE WEEK A YEAR

The sun is setting
in hues of purple and red.
Your thin legs fold up
underneath your body,
trying to stay warm
in the cooling evening air.
It's hard to remember just
how your skin burned
earlier today
under the blazing sun
as you ran full speed
down the old wooden dock.
It creaked beneath your small weight
before you launched awkwardly into the water
trying to cool off.
Dunking quickly under
just before your brother dove in
laughing and splashing.
Mom looking up from her book,
the third one this week,
as she lay catching the rays of the sun
on the other end of the old dock.
Looking anything *but* awkward,
a smile curling up the edges of her lips
that were spotted by summer freckles.

Now the summer heat, a memory
as you push closer to the dying fire,
trying to stay warm.
Licking the stickiness from your fingers,
the remains of melted marshmallow
that was cooked crisp over
the previously orange flames.
Something buzzes by your ear and
you swat at the air
trying to scare it away.
Your eyes grow heavy
from content exhaustion.
I watch you from your future,
remembering the summer nights.
The promised week each year
where I felt more happy and childlike
than any other week.
I watch my young self
drift to sleep
in the memory of the past
just before dad leans over and lifts you
like you are nothing more than a doll.
Snuggled in his arms
while he takes you to the safety inside
the small cabin
that sits next to the dying fire.
A loon coos in the distance.
You drift to seep…
and dream
of what would come tomorrow.
Where you will create more memories
just like this
to last the rest of your life.

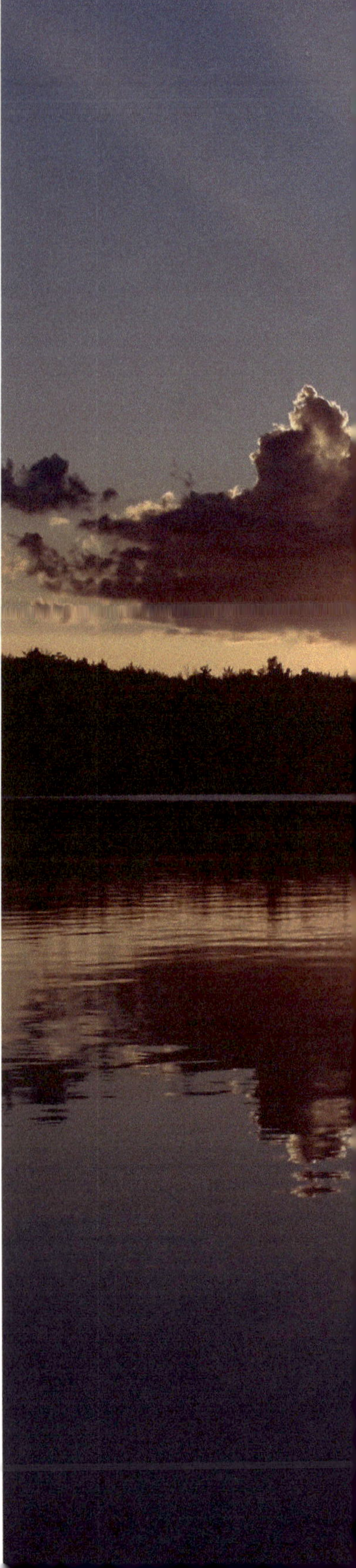

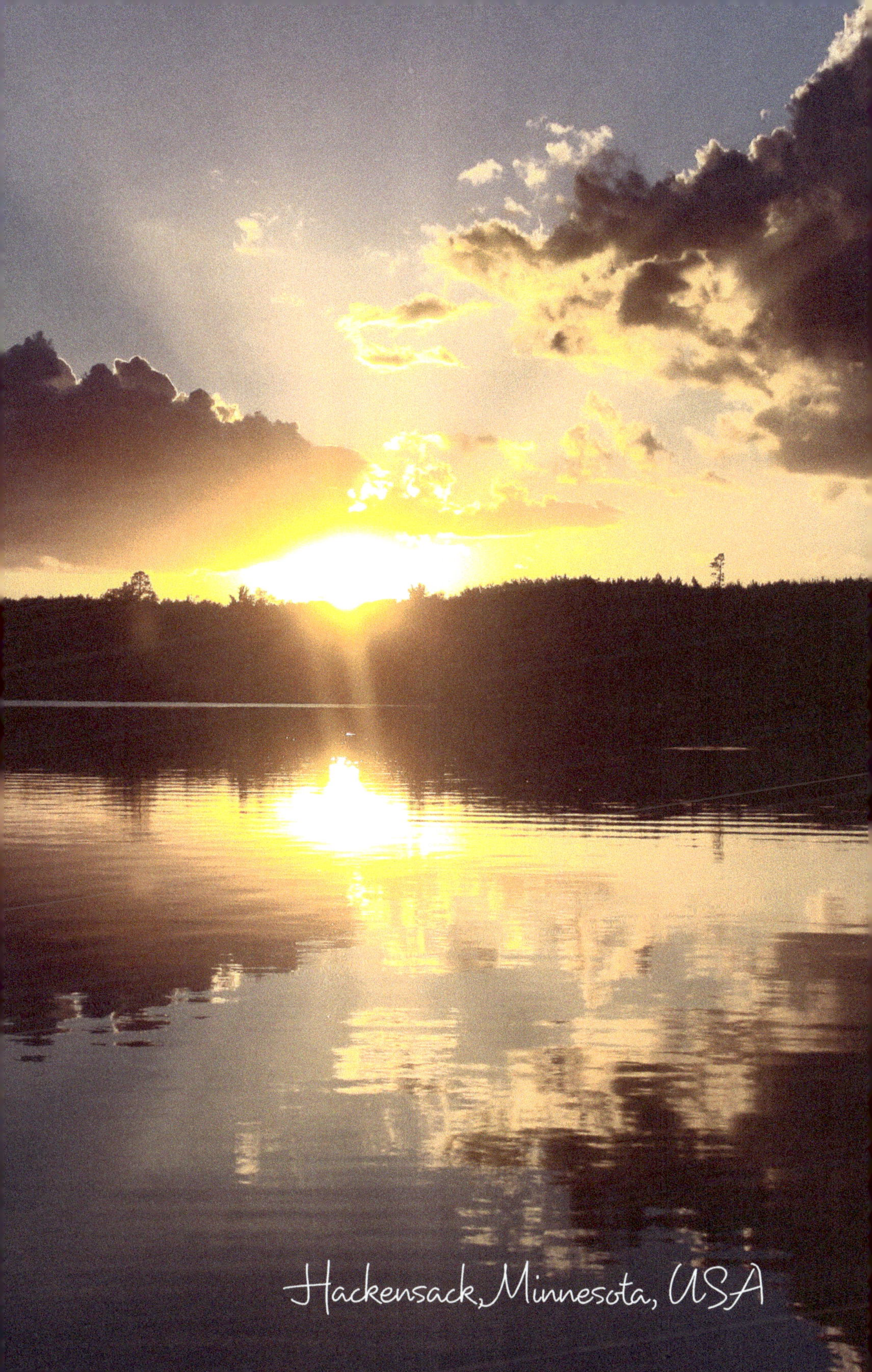
Hackensack, Minnesota, USA

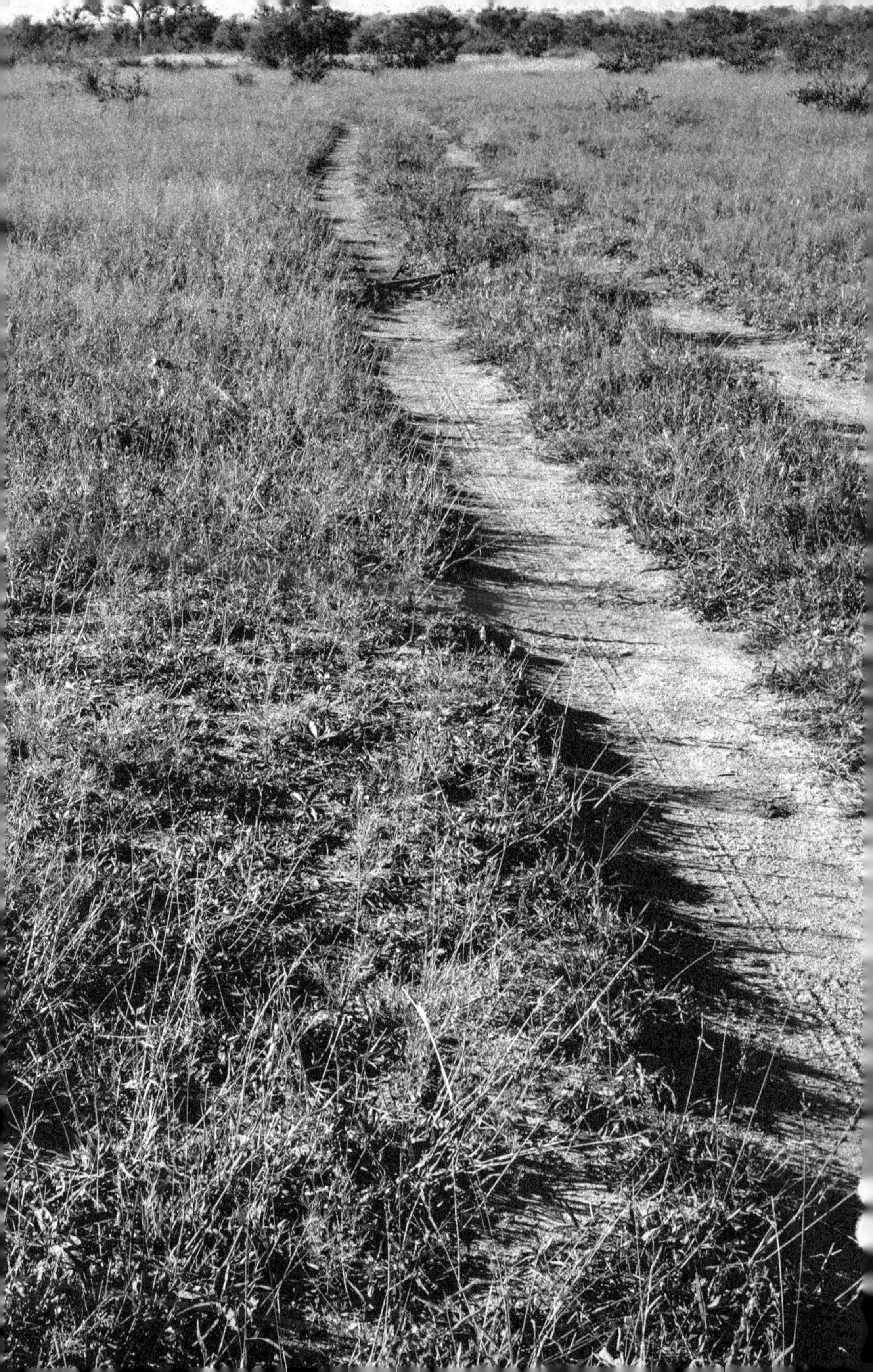

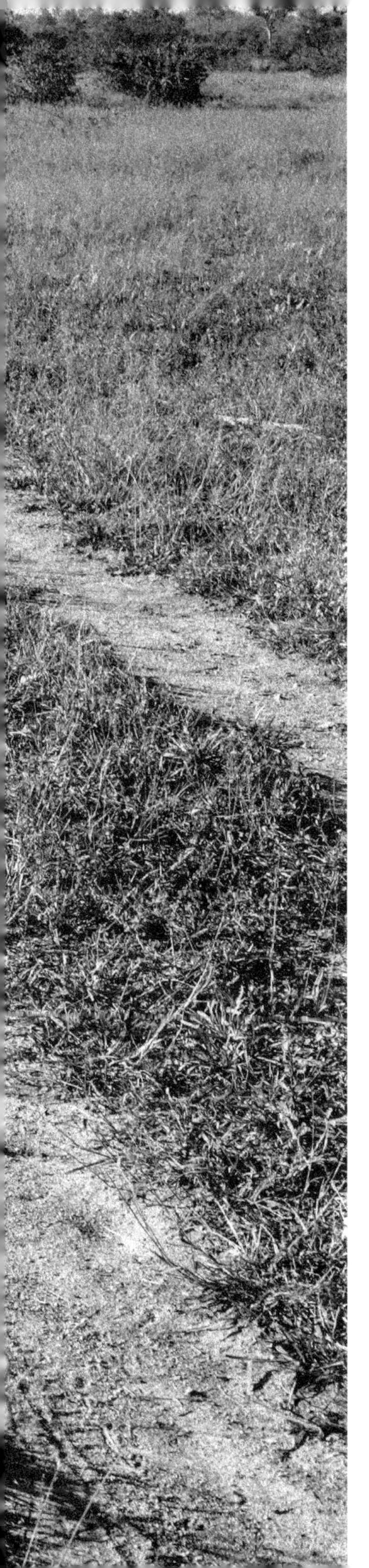

RIOTS AND WINE

here we sit
foreign
in a foreign land
sheltered from the view
enjoying our wine in hand
we sip and converse
our view of civilization
slowly burst
"corrupt"
our new friend says
"they're all corrupt"
through the ages
we quickly learn
the truth behind the lies we see
in this beautiful country
in this beautiful place
we get a lot further
because of our race
and our wallet
he drinks another glass
and shares
the stories that he knows
it's beautiful, yes
this place
sadly beautiful
now families live in shanties
torn from their friends
and their loved ones

jobs taken
given to others
not able to drive
or to educate
it's all who you know
and if you don't know them
you never will
riots driven by
thirst...
for morality
and ethics
and water
we do not learn from the past
the past haunts us
teases us
defines us
people hurt
others thrive
in this unjust world
the divide is vast
between the corrupt
and the rest
we listen in silence
and horror
trying to comprehend
the differences in which we live
and to see
where do we sit?
what can we do?
as we all drink
another glass of wine

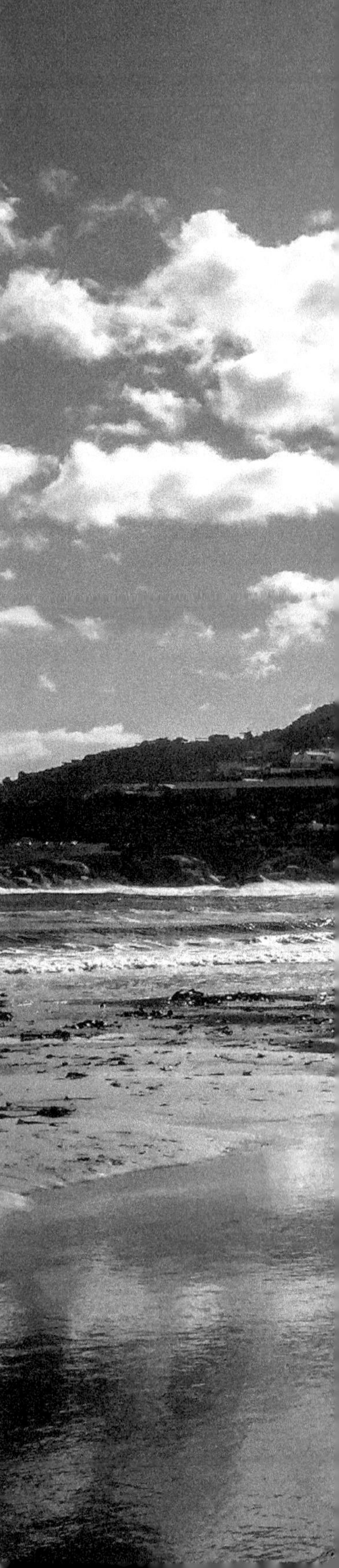

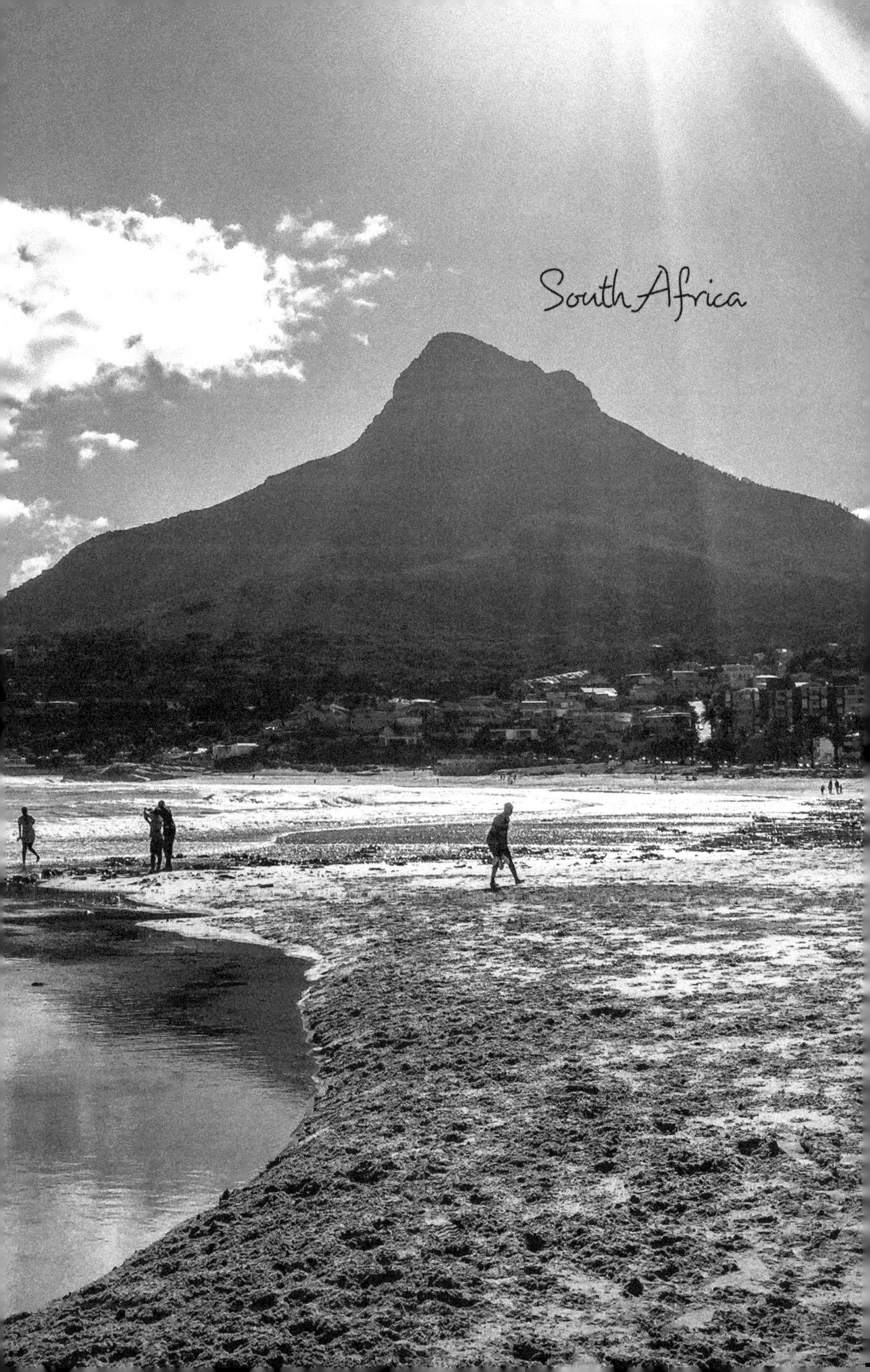
South Africa

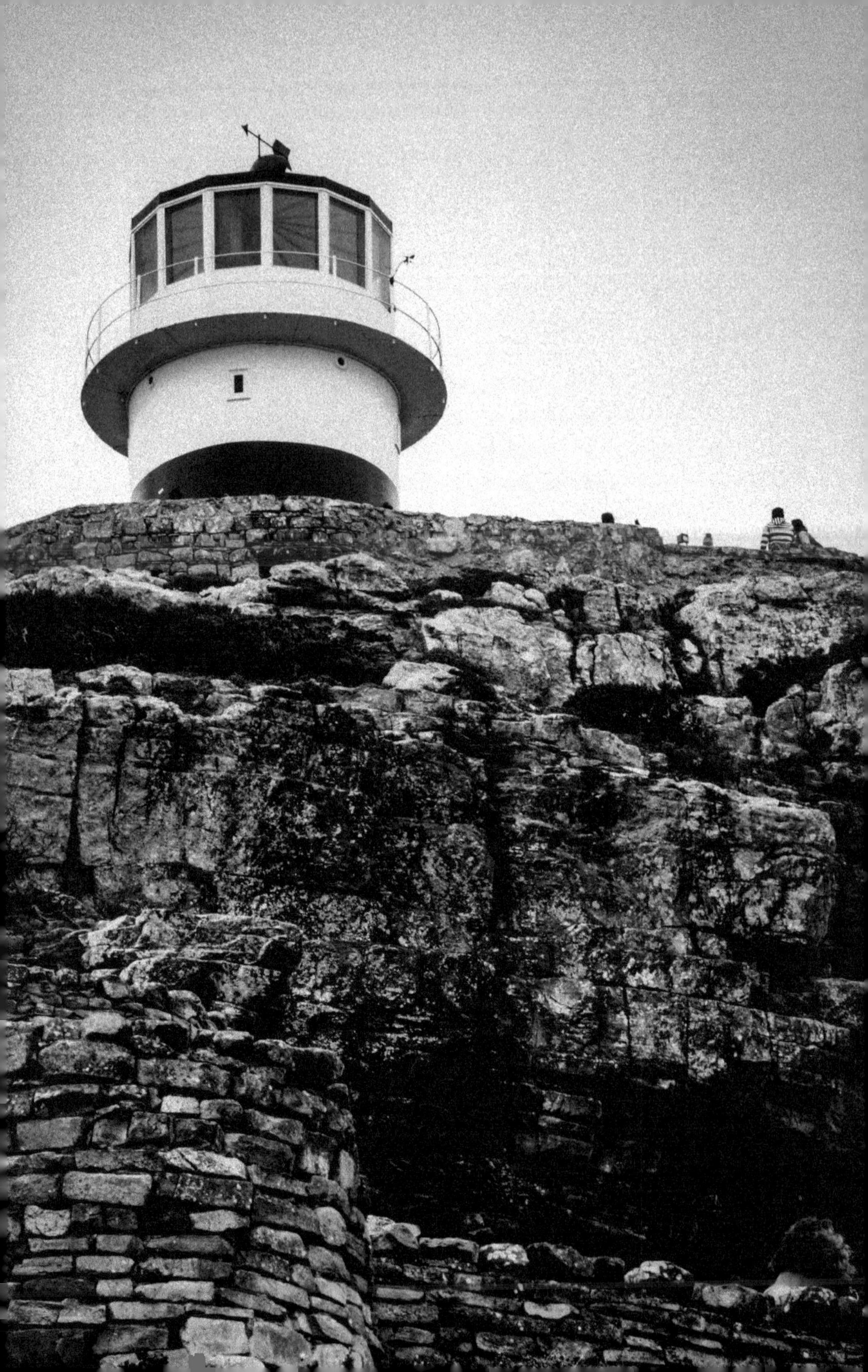

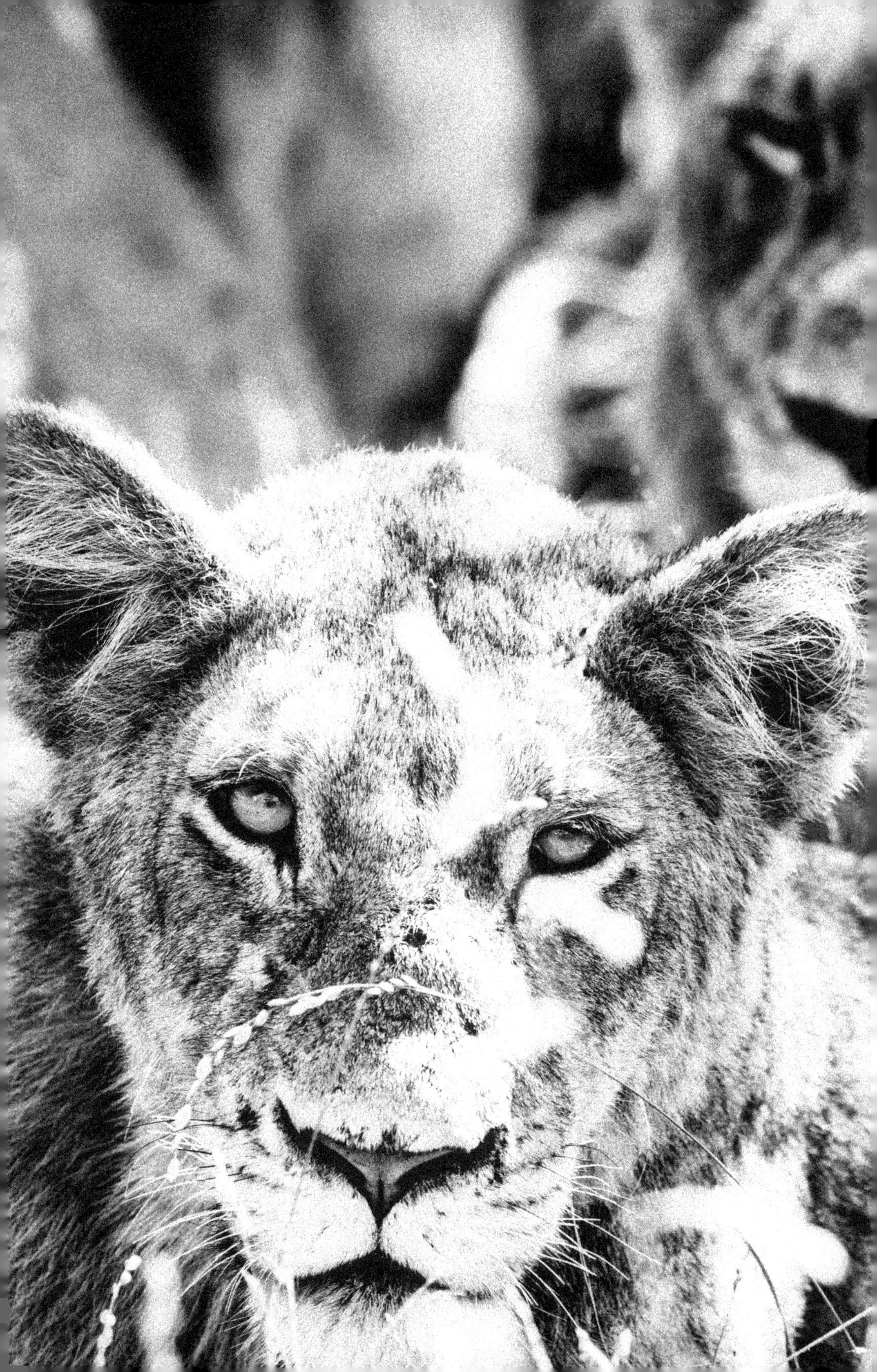

YELLOWSTONE

The snow.
It crunches
beneath the feet
as the girl walks
over it.
Exhilarated
by the frigid cold
and the feeling
of walking on untouched snow
toward s the big brown spot
in the distance.

The snow.
It floats down
from the clouds
that hang heavy
in the sky.
It lands on the eyelashes
of the girl
and she laughs
as she wipes it away
so she can see
the bright land around her.

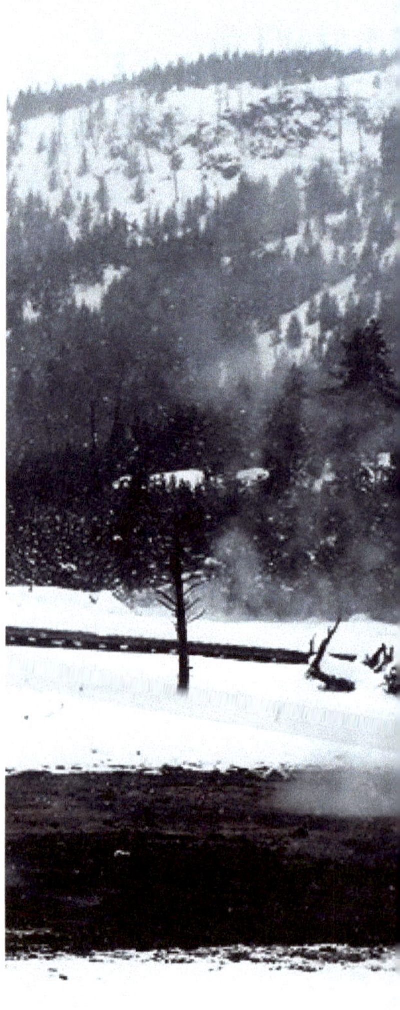

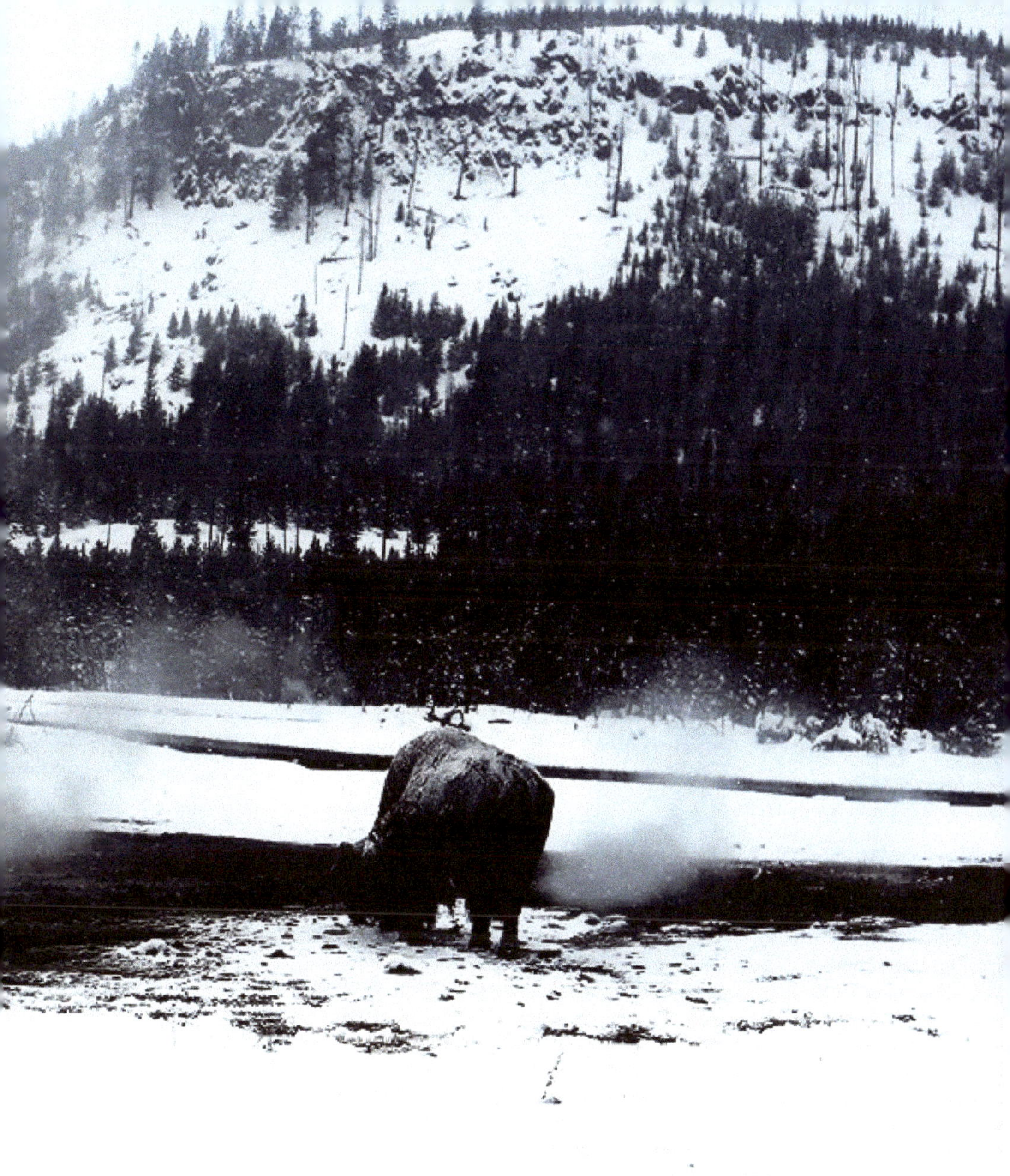

Yellowstone, Wyoming, USA

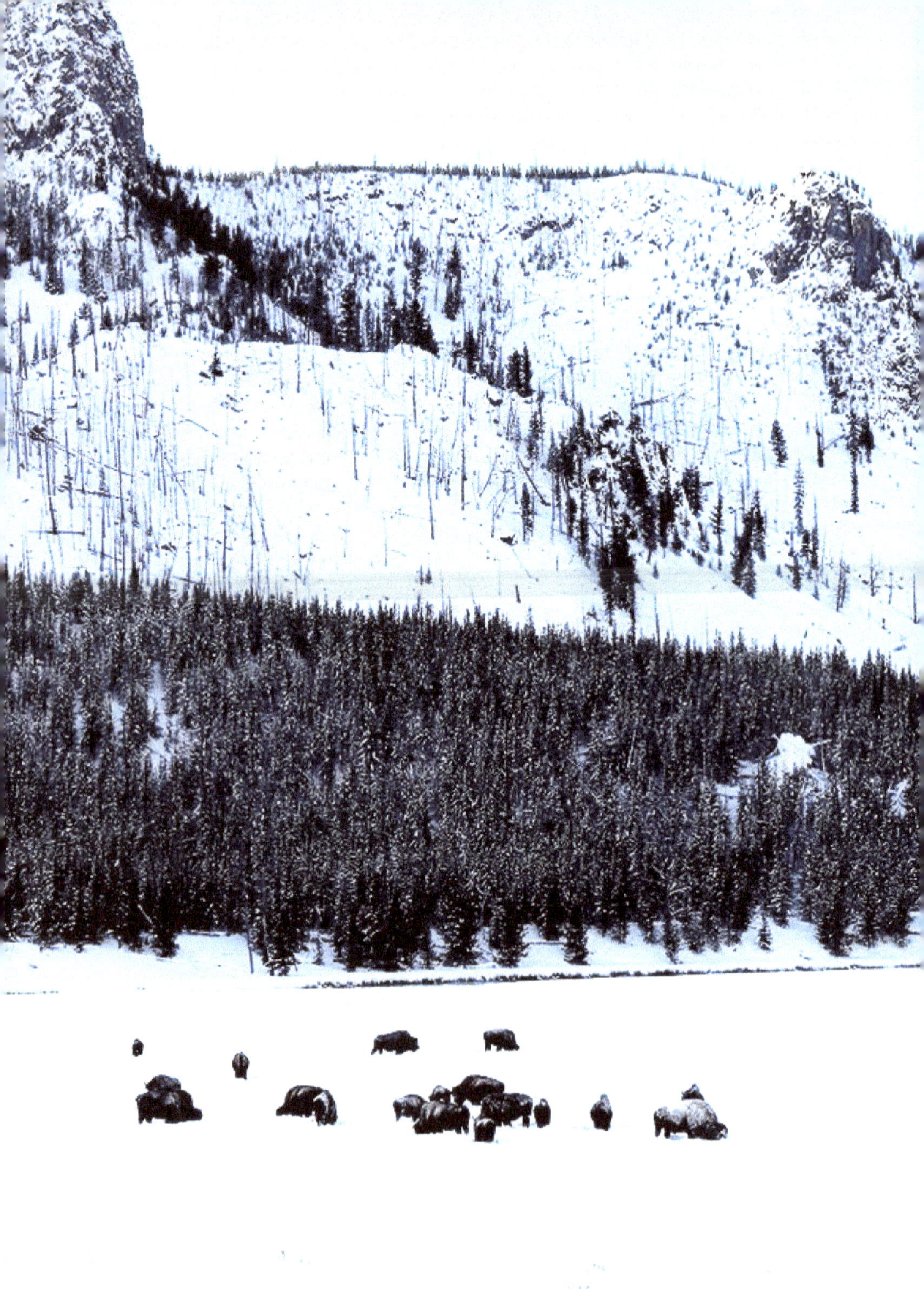

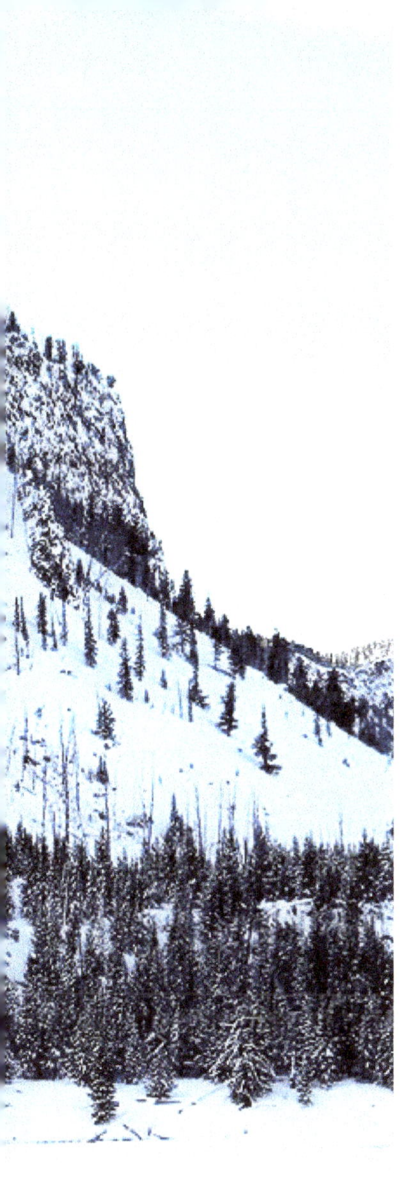

The snow.
It melts in the
dark warm fur
of the bison,
standing alone
on the patch of white.
Pushing his heavy foot
into the ground.
Looking for food.
Not noticing the girl
watching him from afar.

The snow.
It covers the land
with a blanket
of pale clean white.
Reflecting the bright sun.
Hiding the beauty
that people travel to see
with a new view
that still appeals to the select few.
The adventurers
like the shivering, happy girl.

THE MAZE

RIGHT
RIGHT
LEFT
RIGHT
SHIT

RIGHT
LEFT
RIGHT
RIGHT
SHIT

LEFT
RIGHT
LEFT
LEFT
SHIT

LEFT
LEFT
LEFT
RIGHT
SHI....

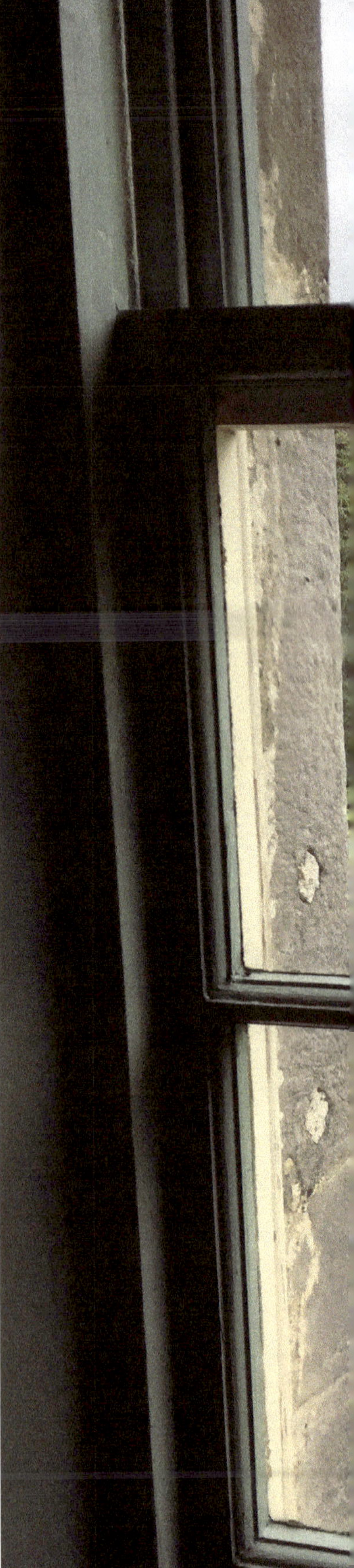

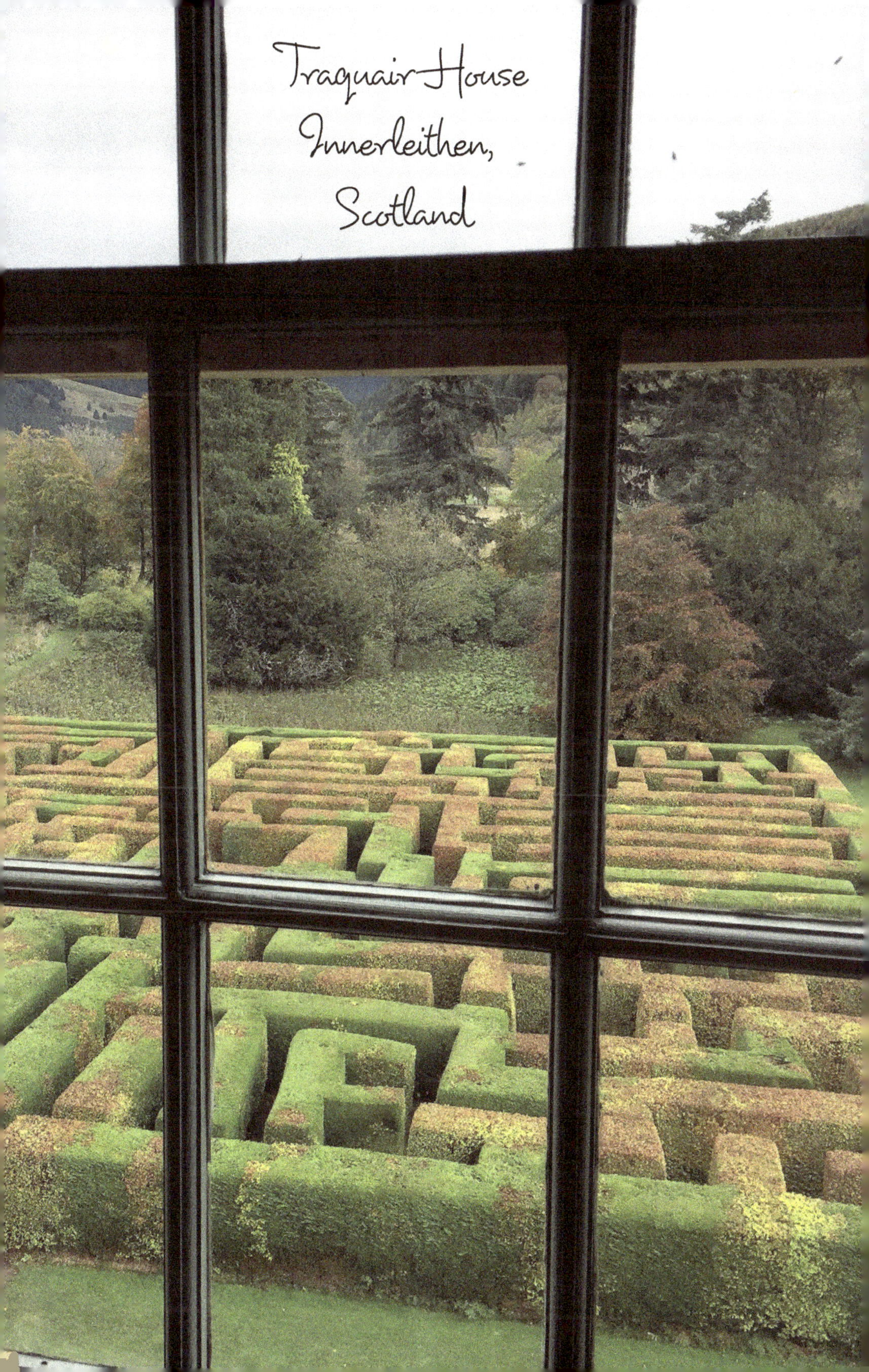

Traquair House
Innerleithen,
Scotland

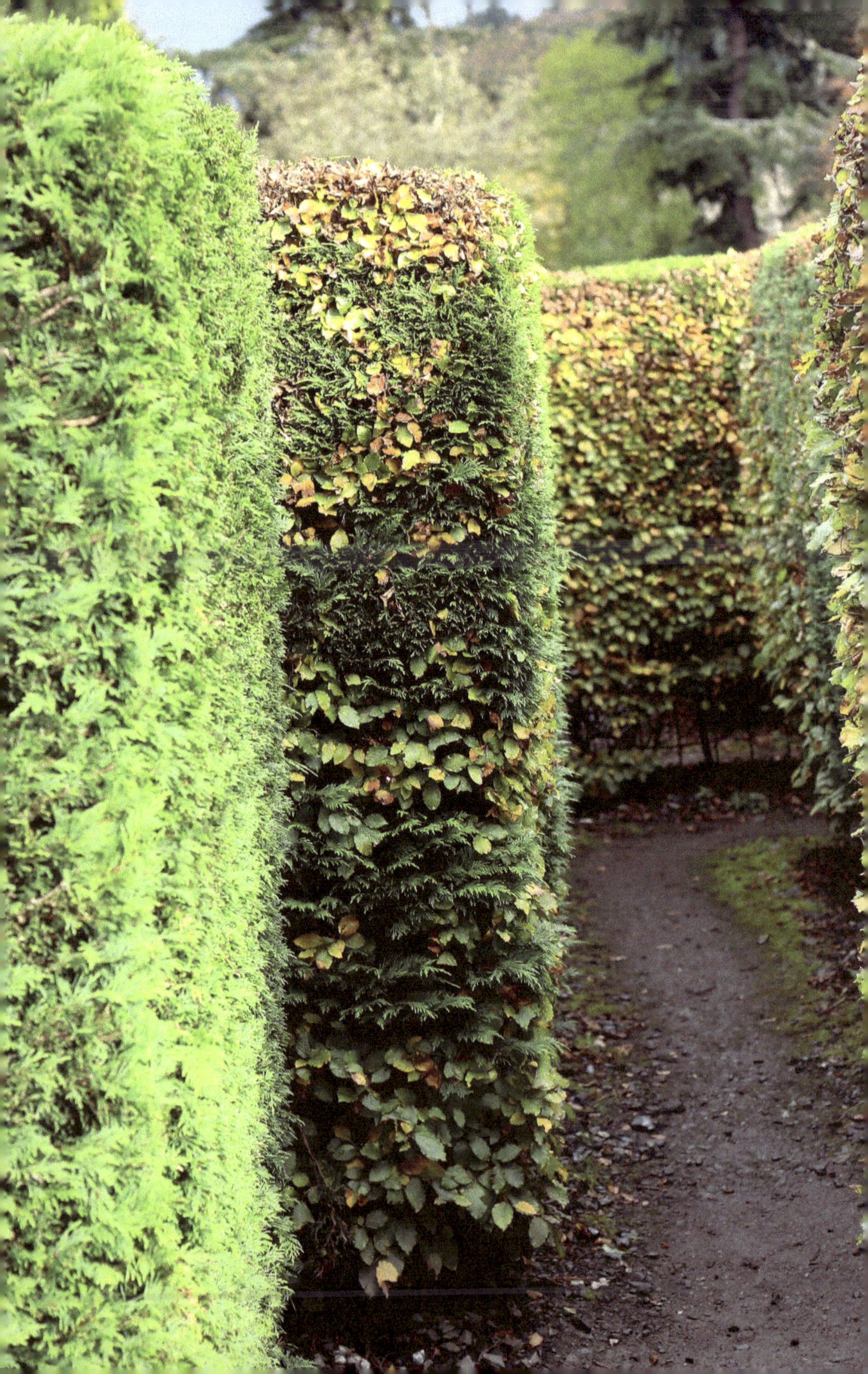

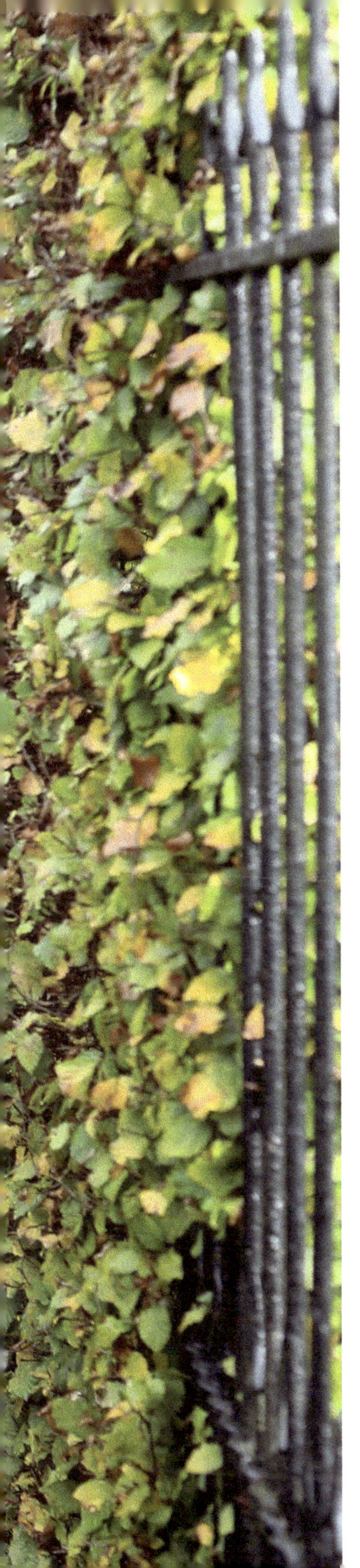

WAIT…

THIS IS IT

WE'VE DONE IT

WE WIN

WE'RE THE CHAMPIONS

IT LASTED FOREVER

IT WAS UNATTAINABLE

BUT HERE WE ARE

WE FOLLOWED THE PATH

WE FOLLOWED THE LUSH GREEN WALLS

THE DEAD ENDS

THE FALSE STARTS

BIRDS CHIRPED ABOVE

MOCKING OUR MISTAKES

BUT HERE

HERE WE ARE

THE GOAL ACHIEVED

THE SUMMIT REACHED

WE FOUND IT

THE CENTER OF THE WORLD

NO

THE UNIVERSE

THE CENTER OF THE HEDGE MAZE

THE BIRDS CHEER AND SOAR ABOVE

AND THEN…

THE SILENCE SETS IN

ALONE

IN THE CENTER…

HOW DO WE GET OUT?

SHIT.

SCATTERED

The smell of gasoline lingers in the air.
I can taste it on my tongue.
The scent of dull smoke
from the hand-rolled cigarettes
of the people standing out of the open door.
The foreign sounds surround us
of the voices of friends talking.
The blue of the water
shining as we fly over it.
Rocks jutting out of the wet,
scattered through the sea and
dotted by the tiny white houses.
An hour…
or two.
From a bustling city of people in a hurry
to a small island filled with calm,
as we speed in a sea plane
to an island,
placed randomly
by God
in the middle of the blue,
blue,
sea.

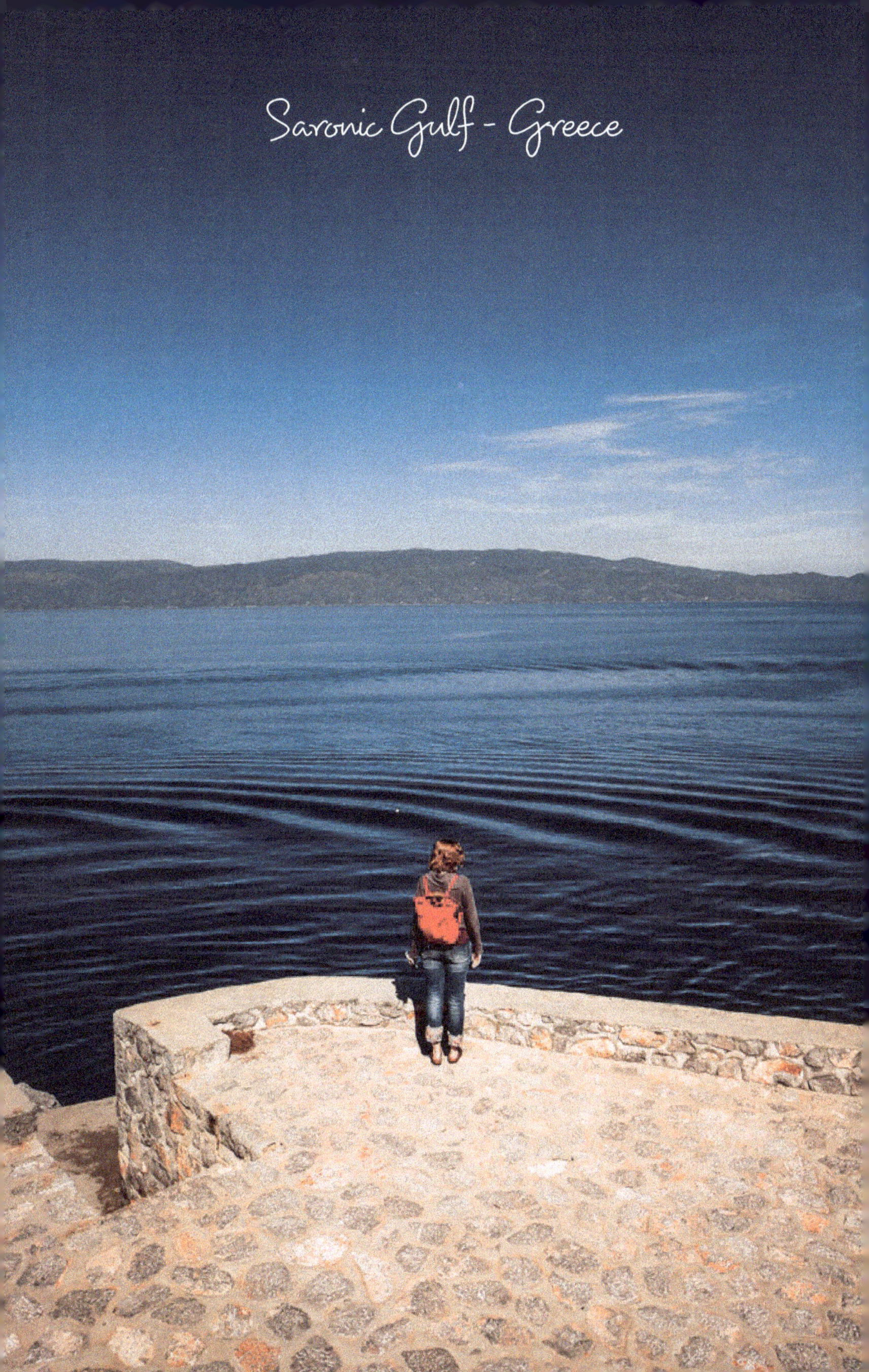
Saronic Gulf - Greece

A FAR CRY

Pass through an archway made of stone
and carved with care and love
for a man called Isa Khan Niazi alone

A noble of the past
built while he still lived
in a time when the rich saw all and amassed

More money than they needed
while the poor starved in the streets
like today, they pleaded

The buildings are complex and beautiful
visited by those who pay a fee
the majesty of the place is irrefutable

The sounds of outside slip away
honks
yells
laughter
music
fade
a hot breeze blows and the trees sway

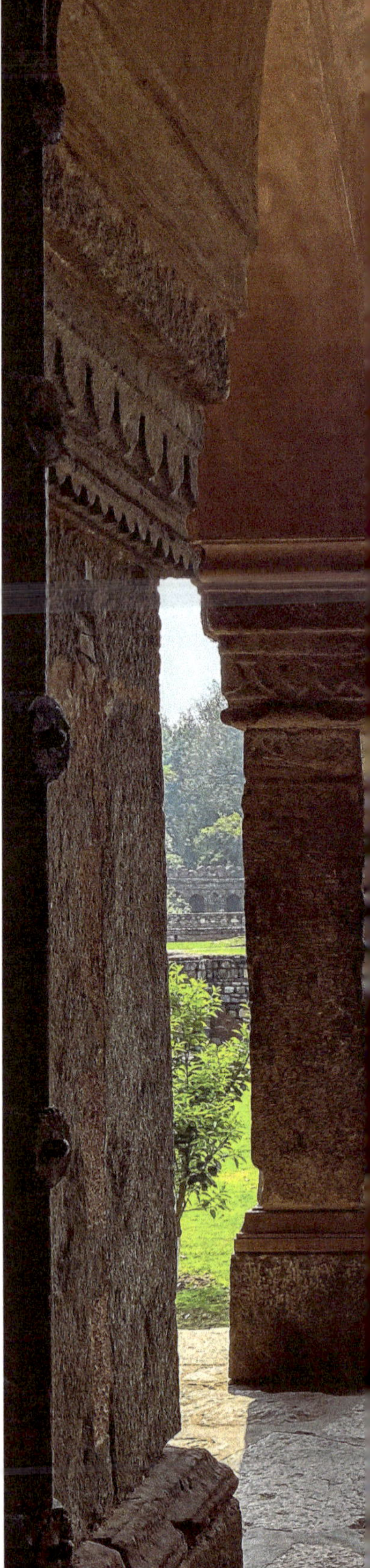

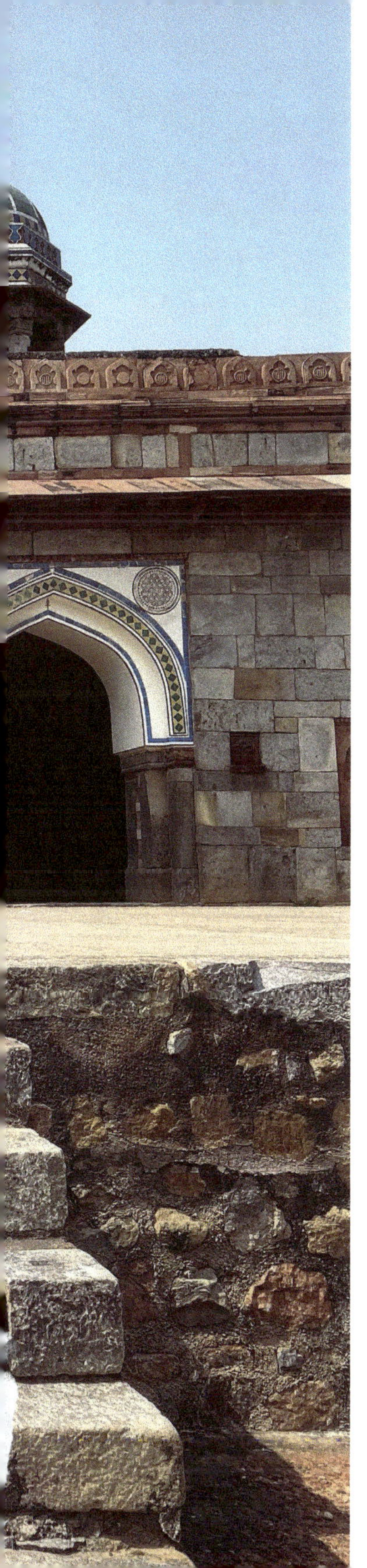

This place, it almost feels like a dream
everything so manicured and structured
the blue tiles sparkle, or so it would seem

Such a far cry
from the wonderful chaos outside
but the peace is hard to deny

You forget the troubles of others
for just a short moment
eyes wide, taking in the still bright colors

Bare toes flexing against the stone floor
you remember this isn't real life
this calm place built years before

So, the sounds return with their full flair
as you pass back through an archway made of stone
and carved with care

MOTHER

The sun shines above,
a spotlight in the sky,
blocked by not a single cloud of white or grey.
Its glare focuses down on us
as we walk
slowly
silently
safely.
I'm bookended by two formidable men,
formidable by what lays easily in their hands.
Their guns are held casually.
Never having used them,
I'm hoping today is not the first.
We walk through the prickly bush and out onto a rock,
tan and large.
I sit
warming like a lizard.
They stand,
my guards.
We squint and peer
into the grey water
that is rushing beside us
Where?
Where?
There.
The water is beading
off the leathery broad shoulders
that sit just above the line.
rippling the smooth surface.
Two holes protrude
and blow bubbles into the air.
Beyond the nostrils
two bottomless eyes.
She freezes,
her eyes meeting mine.

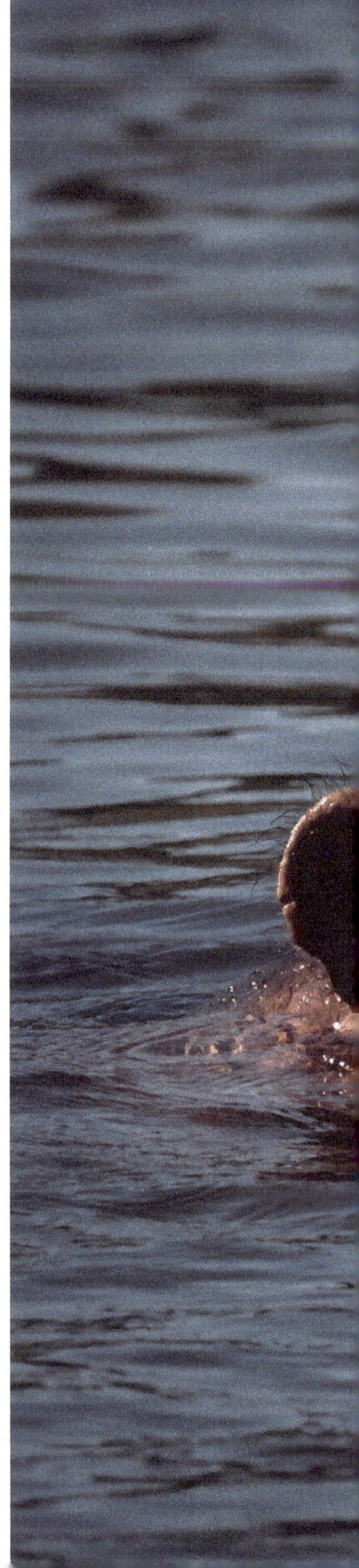

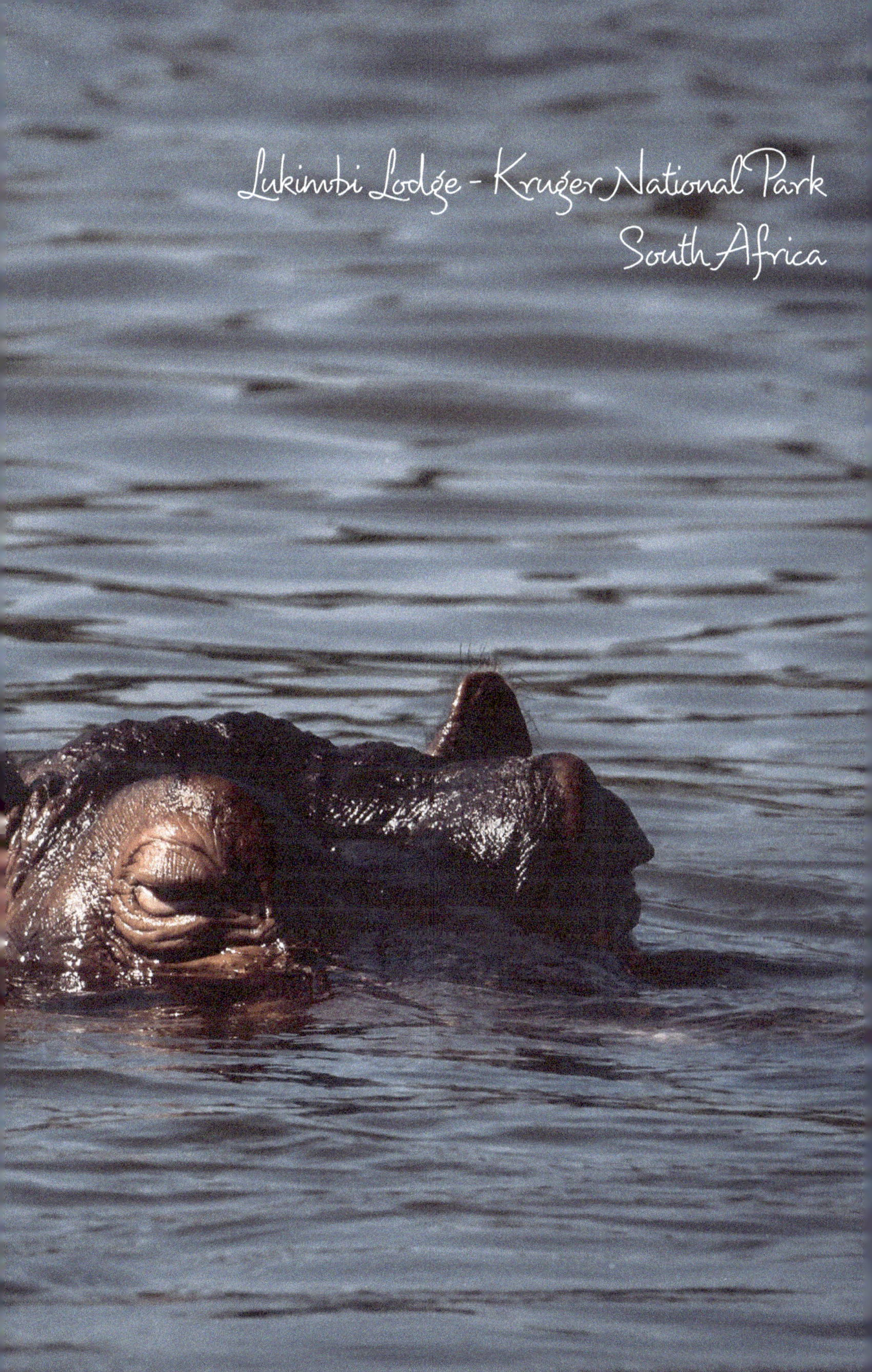
Lukimbi Lodge - Kruger National Park
South Africa

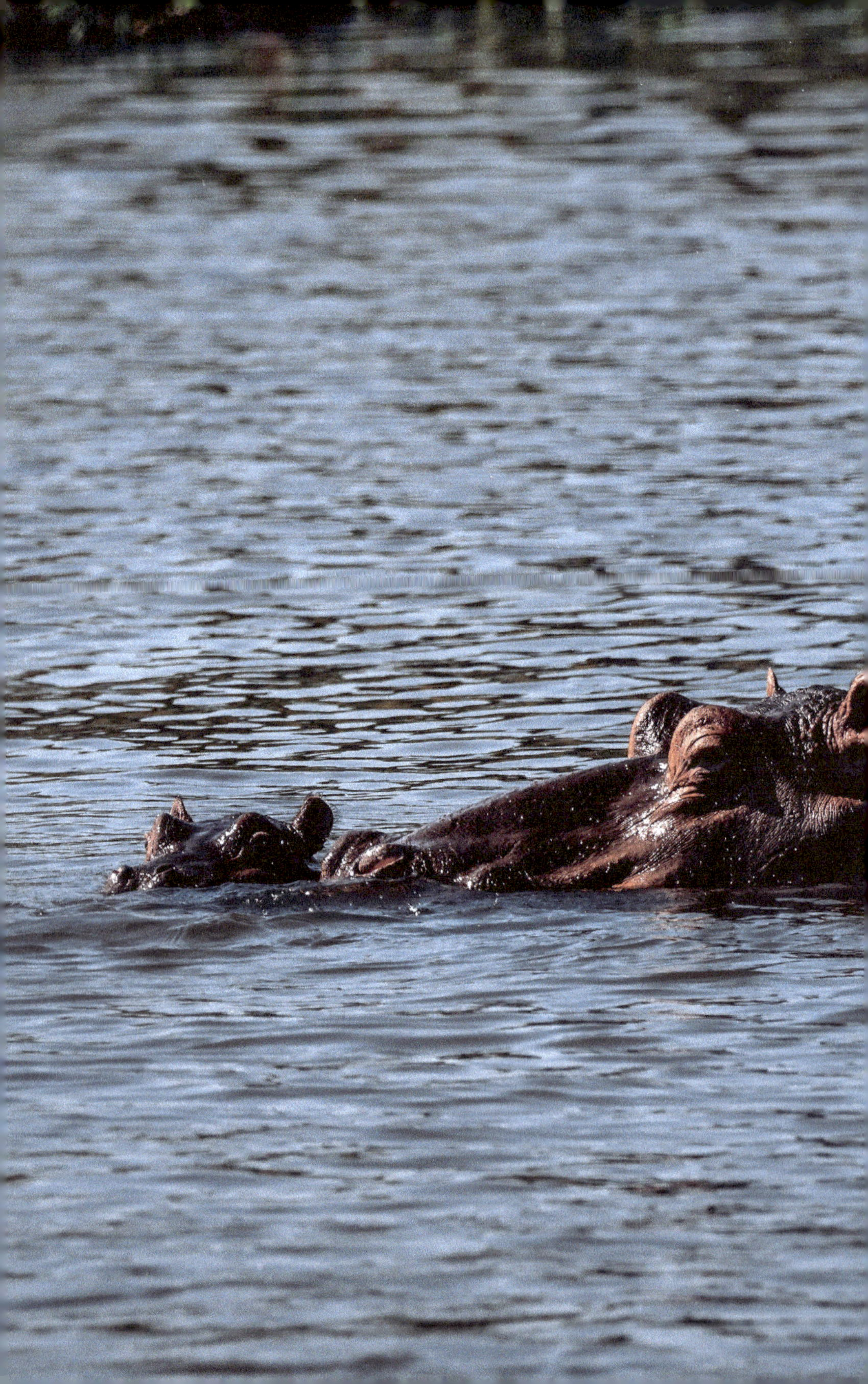

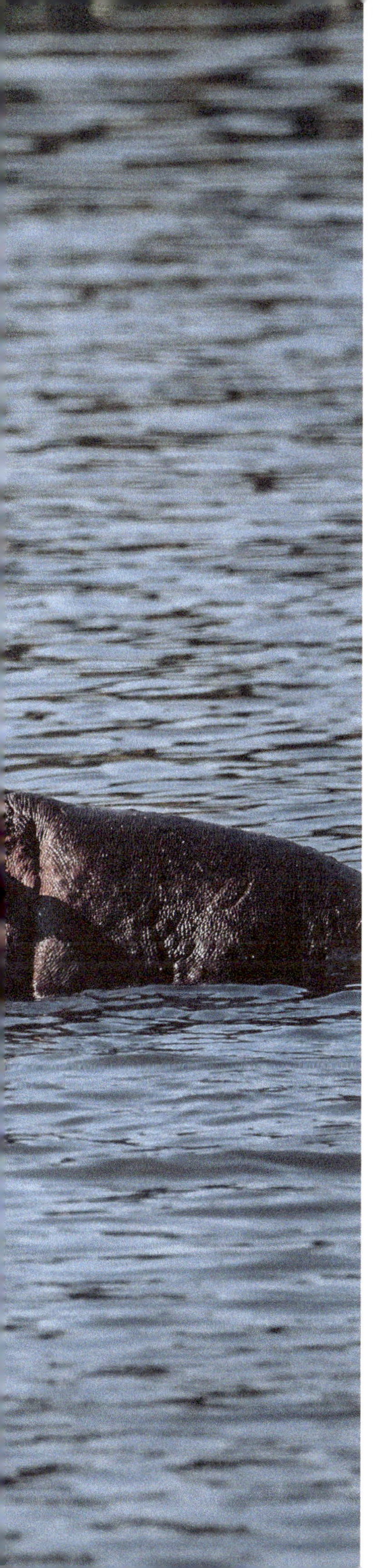

Every muscle in my body strains
to hold myself in place
as I meet her stare,
not wanting to break contact.
Her life is there
in her eyes,
protective
of her home,
her land.
I see strength
and loyalty
and danger.
She doesn't want me to forget
she is king and queen.
I see movement.
My eyes flicker away
to her mirror image,
her miniature mirror
paddling next to her.
I breathe out
not realizing I had been holding in air for so long.
The baby
that the mother protects.
I look back into her eyes
with a new understanding.
Her heavy lids drop down
for a moment.
She blinks
before taking a slow
graceful
step
towards the rock
I am sitting on.
The men motion towards the bush.
I stand.
They bookend me again
as I glance once more
behind me into the endless brown eyes.

THE GODS

Standing where they stood
before Christ was born.
The Gods of our ancestors.
A foot set down by Athena
to create the pale city below.
The bright sun shines in daggers of gold
lighting the blue sky
and the pillars made of marble
that were carried up the hill on the backs
of slaves
over a thousand years ago.
The faces of stone show the sadness
of gods forgotten.
Now just a memory evolved
into the gods we know today.
The air is sweet
and quiet
before the school groups and busses
show up to join our "ooos" and "ahhhs"
at the thought of the gods that once lived
in the minds of all of those around them.
My eyes drift up
and up
and up
to stare into the eyes
of the worn-out women and men
carved into the marble.
I close my eyes.
The sun heats my face
as if I'm kissed by the gods,
and I stand where they stood
all those years ago.

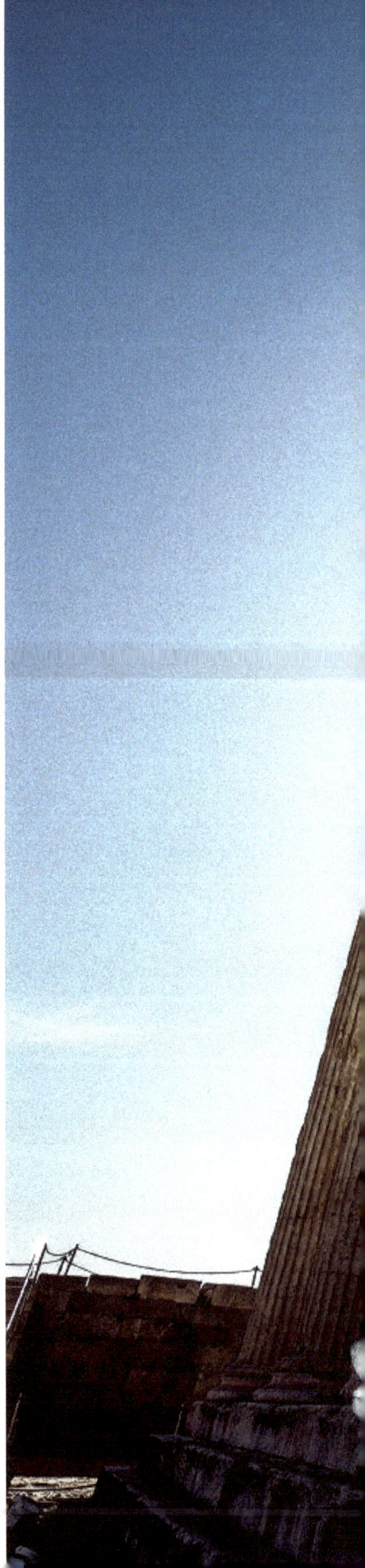

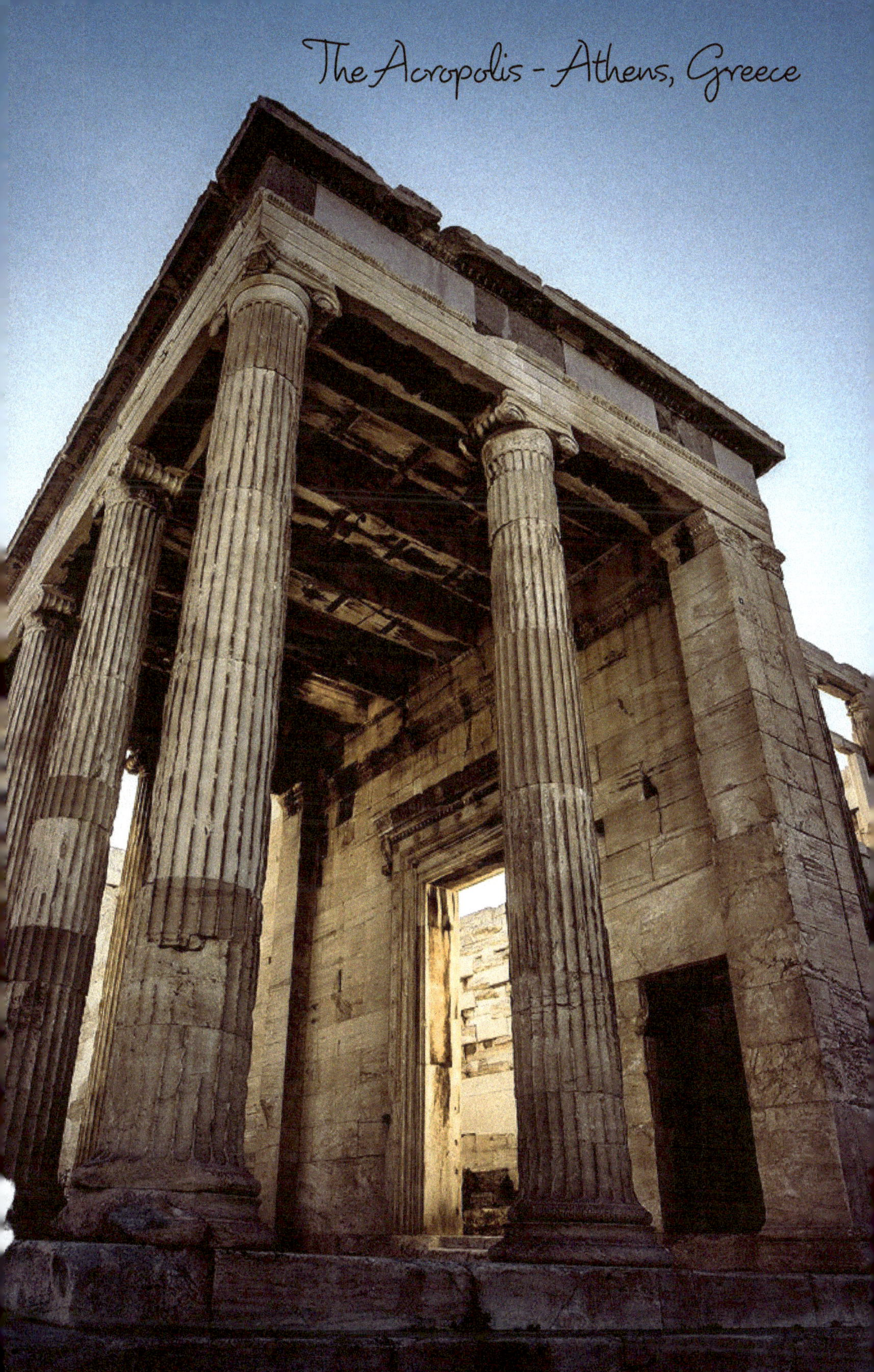
The Acropolis - Athens, Greece

WHERE THE ELVES LIVE

"THERE!"
She points
towards the water
falling off the side of a hill,
then disappearing behind a rock.
She must see where it lands.
Where does the water hide?
Her finger trails down
following the falling water
to the stone below.
"THERE!"
Her eyes widen as she sees a crack.
A crevice.
Hidden in the rock.
Just big enough for a person.
Or two.
She runs towards it,
not noticing the shoelace
of her hiking boot...
unraveling,
waiting to be grabbed by the elves
that live in the cave
that she is running towards.
She squeezes through the opening
eyes adjusting to the deepening darkness.

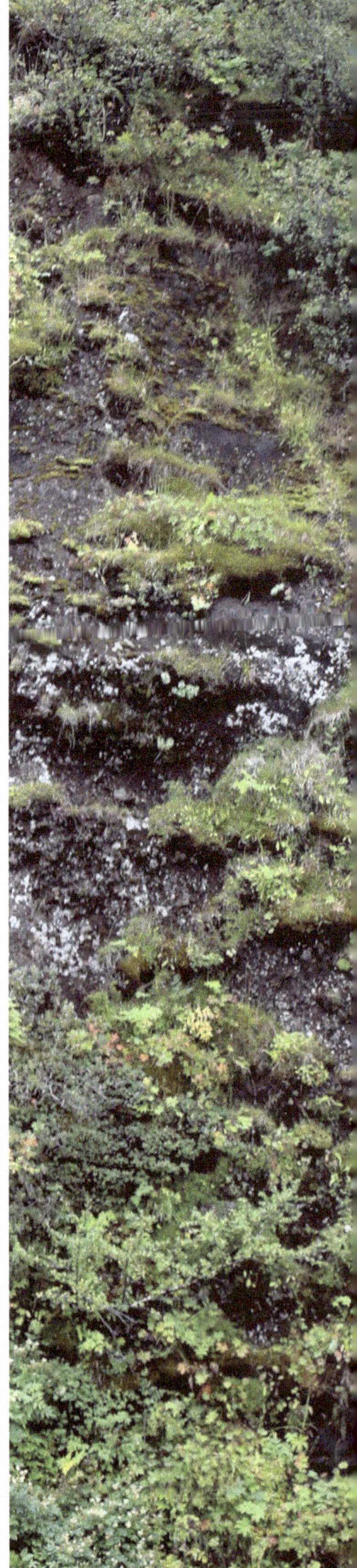

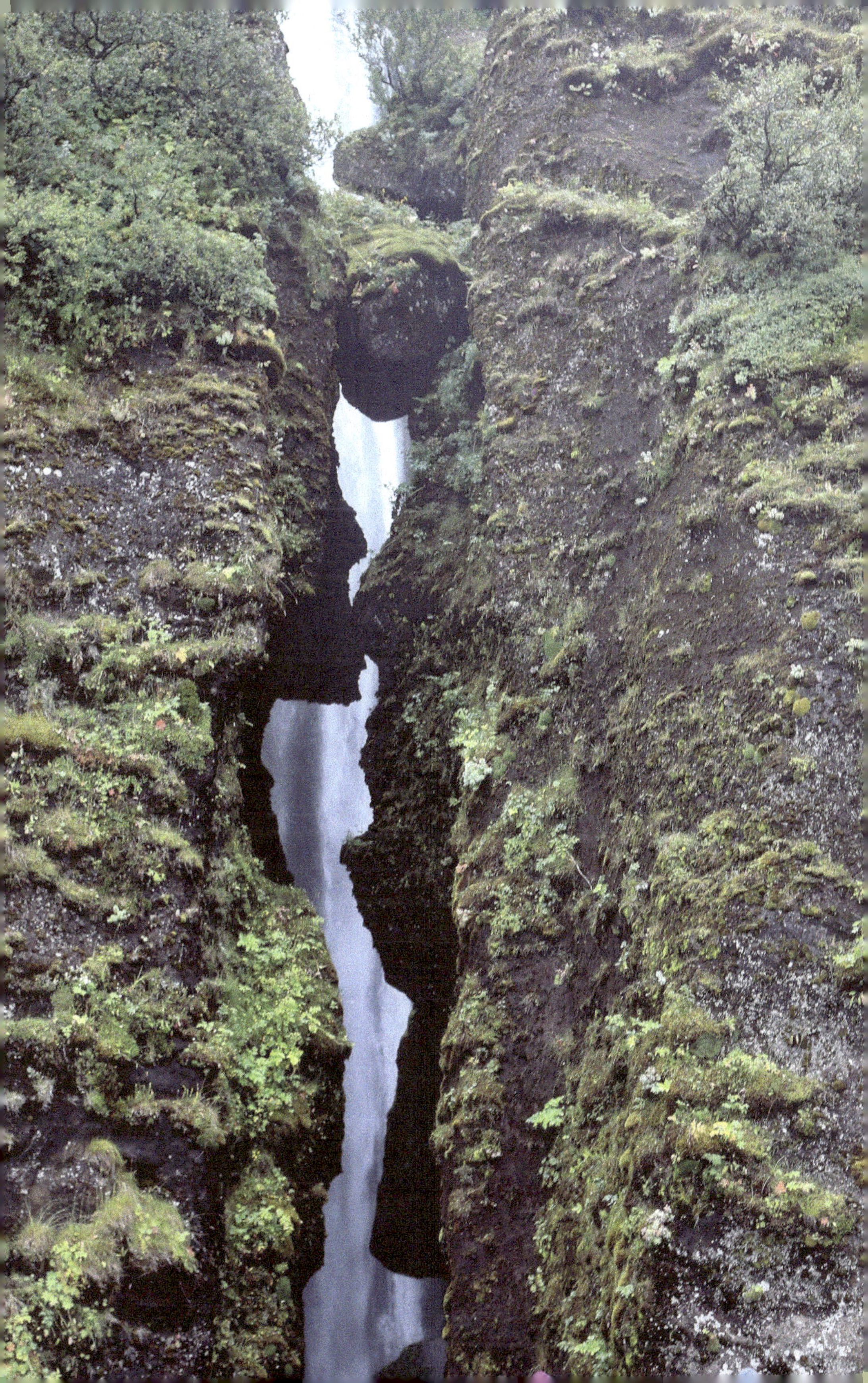

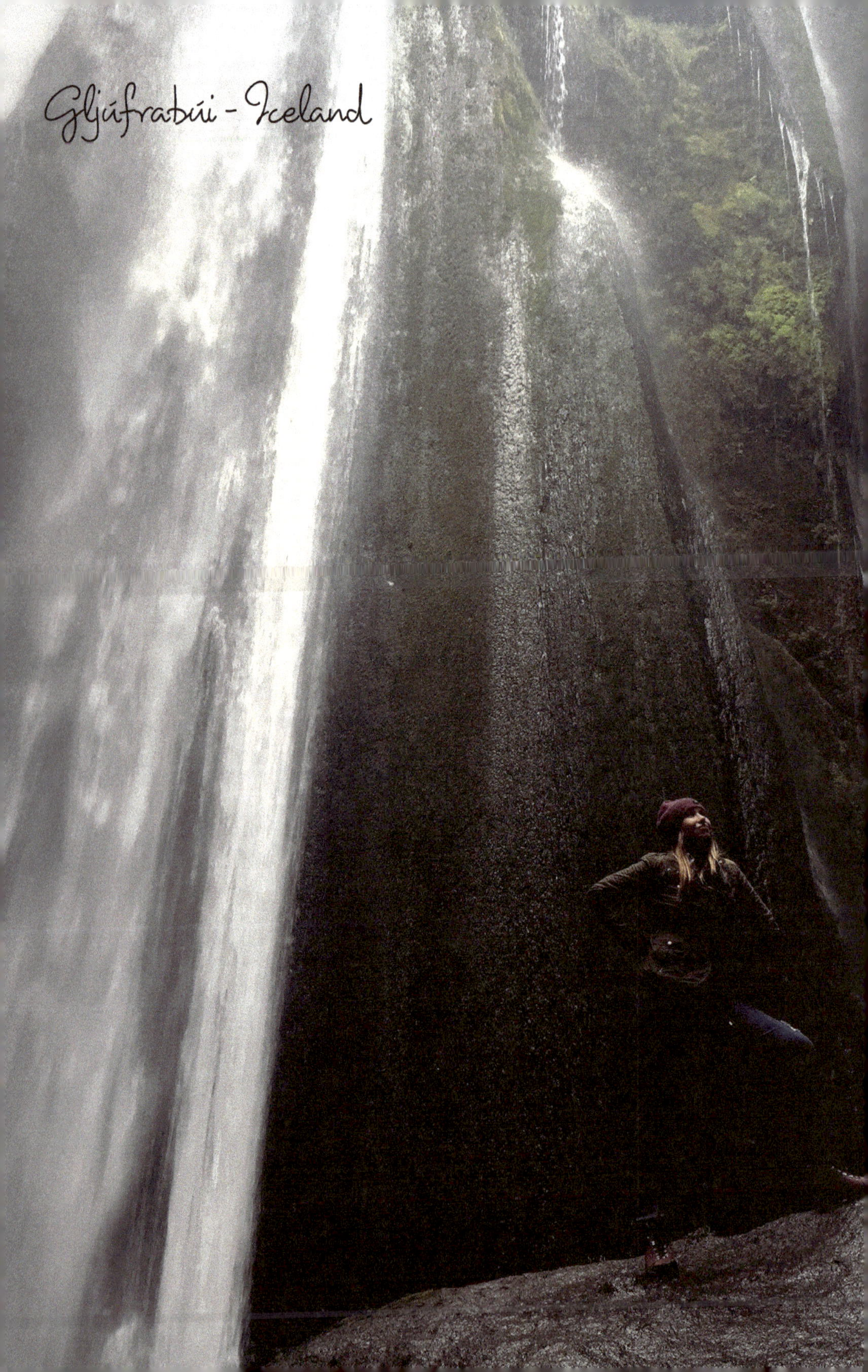
Gljúfrabúi - Iceland

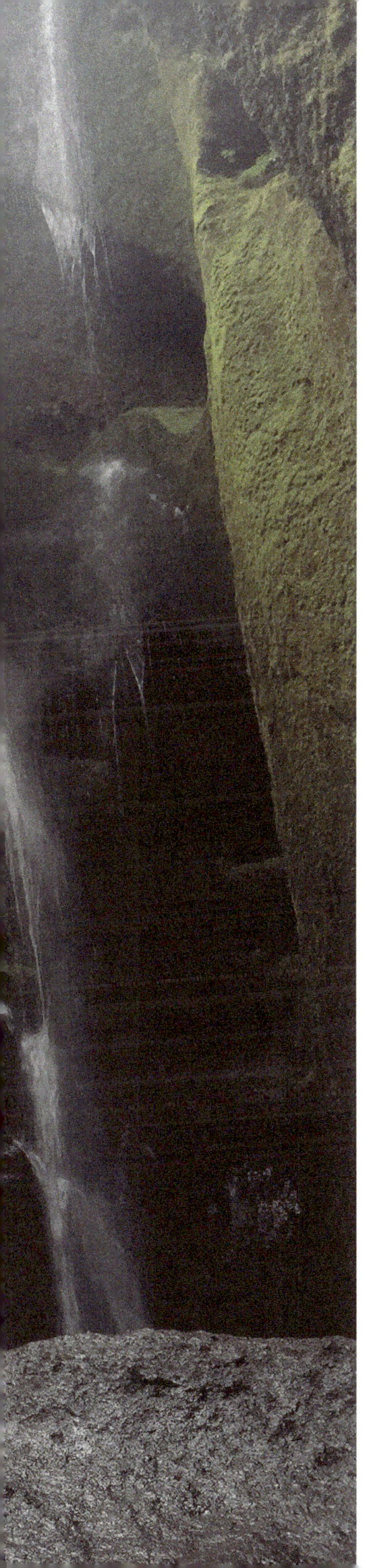

Hugging the wall
away from the stream of water
flowing against the ground.
The eyes of elves
laughing as they watch her
fumbling towards the growing sound
of trickling water.
"THERE!"
Her eyes widen as the walls do.
From crevice to cave
open at the top
to let the water fall in.
It hits the side of the rock and sprays
into the rays of sunlight
and trickles and flows
down the sides of the cave.
She spies a large rock in the middle
and scrambles up it,
marveling at the water falling
all around her.
She smiles back at the elves,
mirroring their happy and mischievous faces
in her own
as she stands
inside a waterfall
feeling like the explorer
she had always dreamed to be.

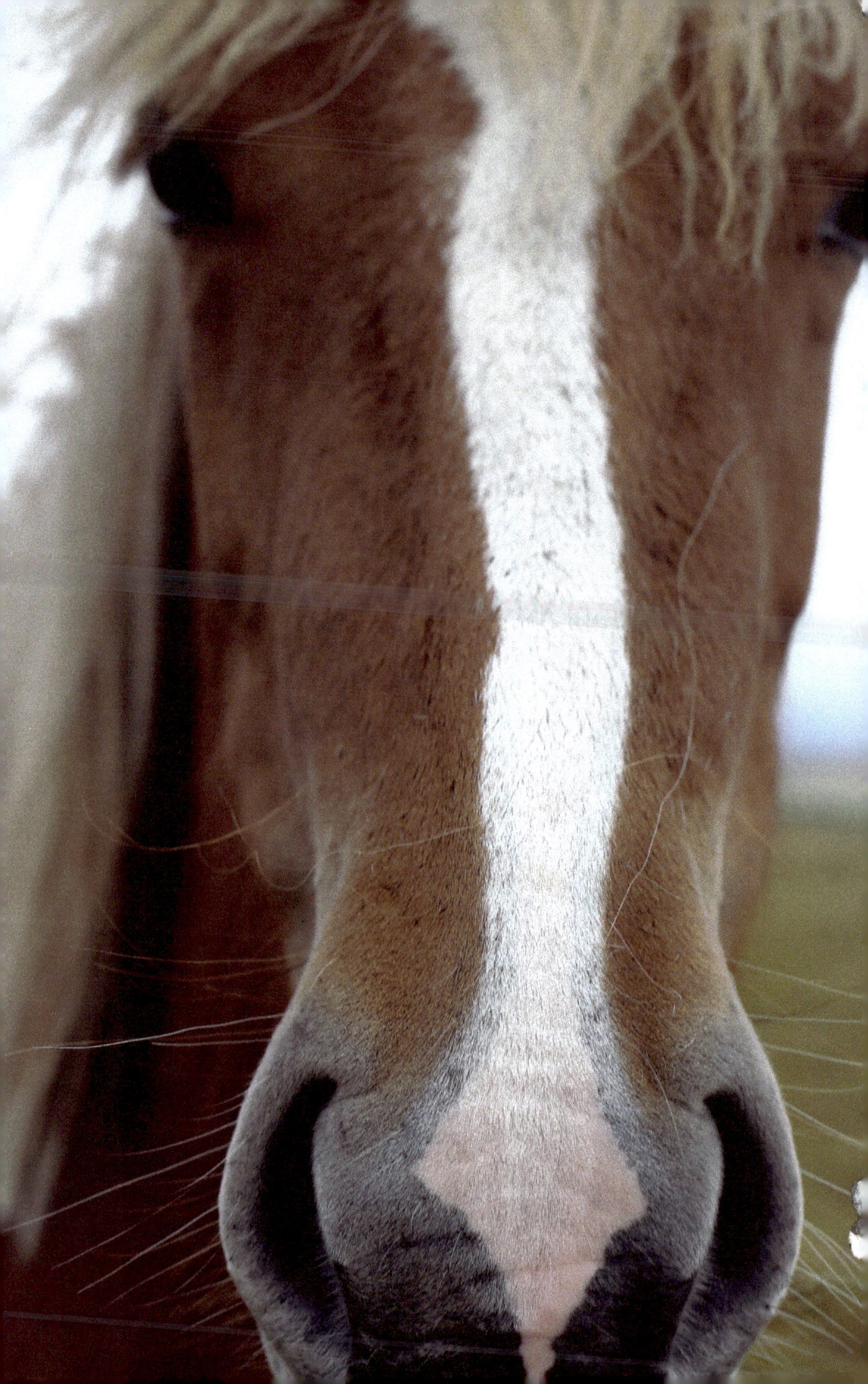

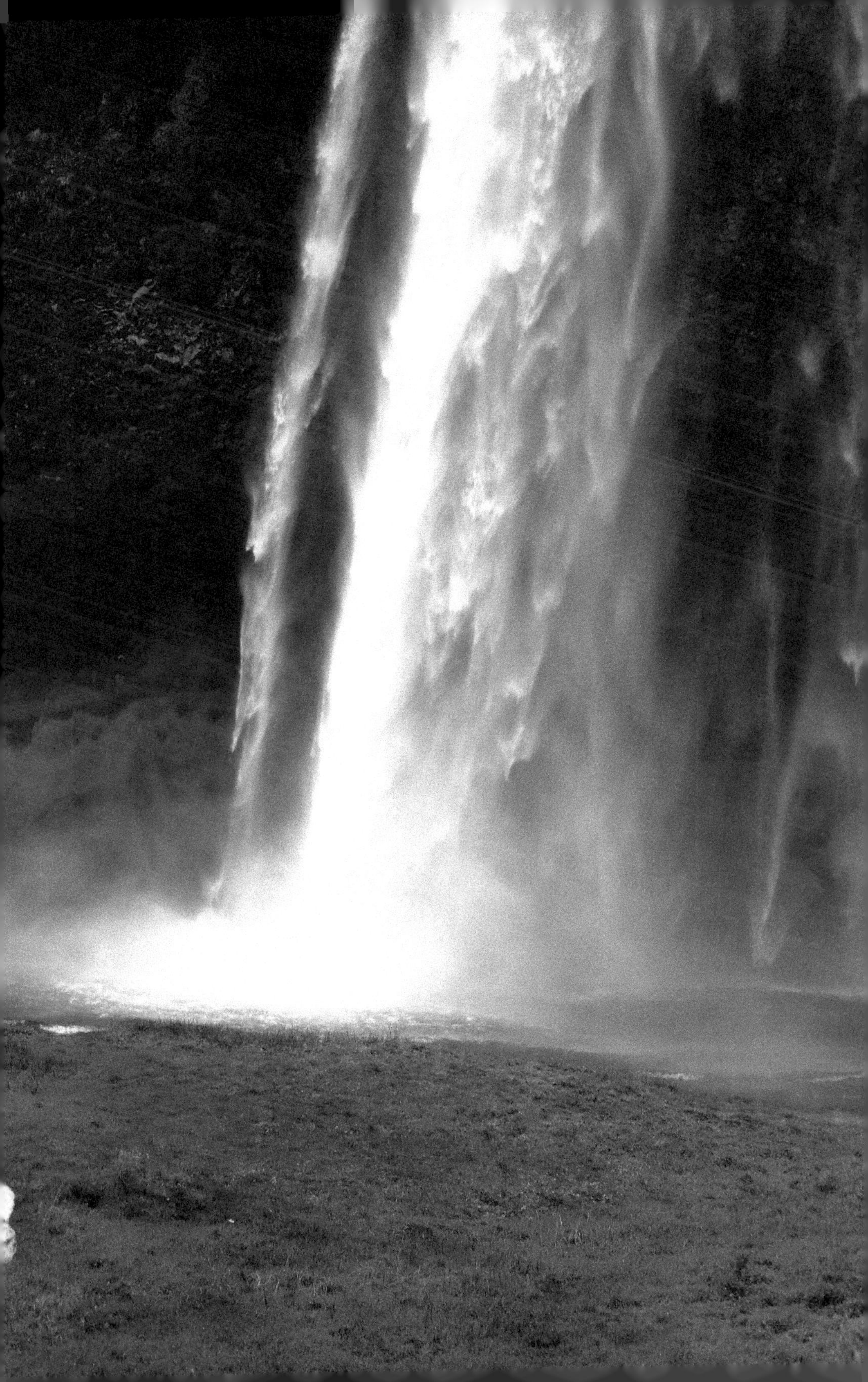

IRISH SEA - CALM

The ocean breathes in;
a small white dot is pushed towards the sky.
Inside the dot – there are people.
Tiny worlds.
The bright blue eyes shining out of the face
of the captain,
searching for the pop of green land.
A girl is there too.
She turns her face up towards the sun
but it doesn't warm her skin.
Skin beaten cold by the ocean spray
and the wind.
The ocean breathes out.
The boat drops.
Ten feet...
Twenty...
Thirty...
The land is gone.
The girl looks down at the water
that slides in the bottom of the boat.
The water slides right;
slides to the left.
Back and forth over the chipped paint
that was once painted pale blue,
like the sea captain's eyes.
The sides of the tiny boats pulsate
against the deep breath of the water.
The girl notices the rust running from
the grey bolts that hold the tiny vessel.
The tiny people all hold their breath,
waiting for the ocean to breathe deep again.
Waiting to be thrust towards the sky.
The surface of the earth.
So that they can see the green again;
a reminder that they are not alone.
A tiny dot in a vast grey wetness...
and the ocean ***BREATHES IN.***

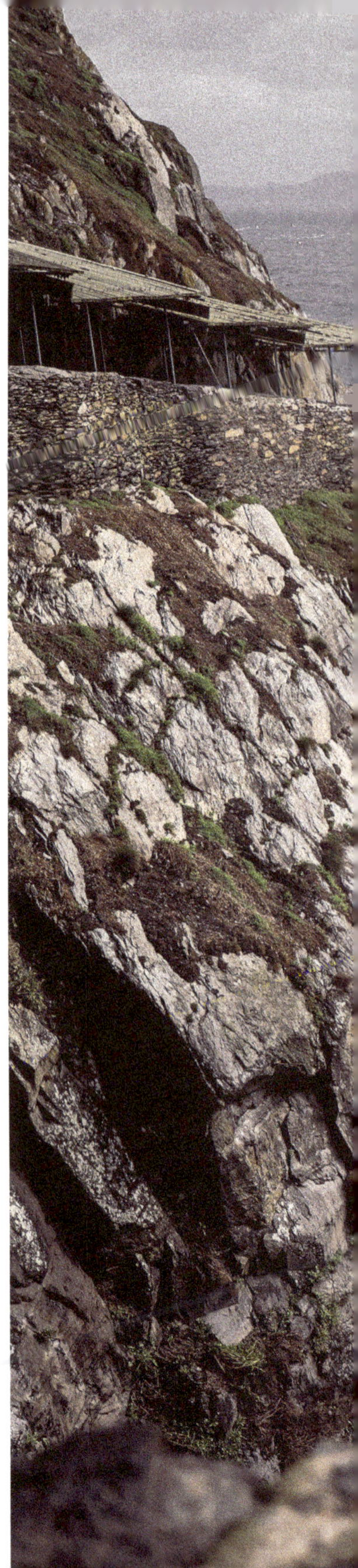

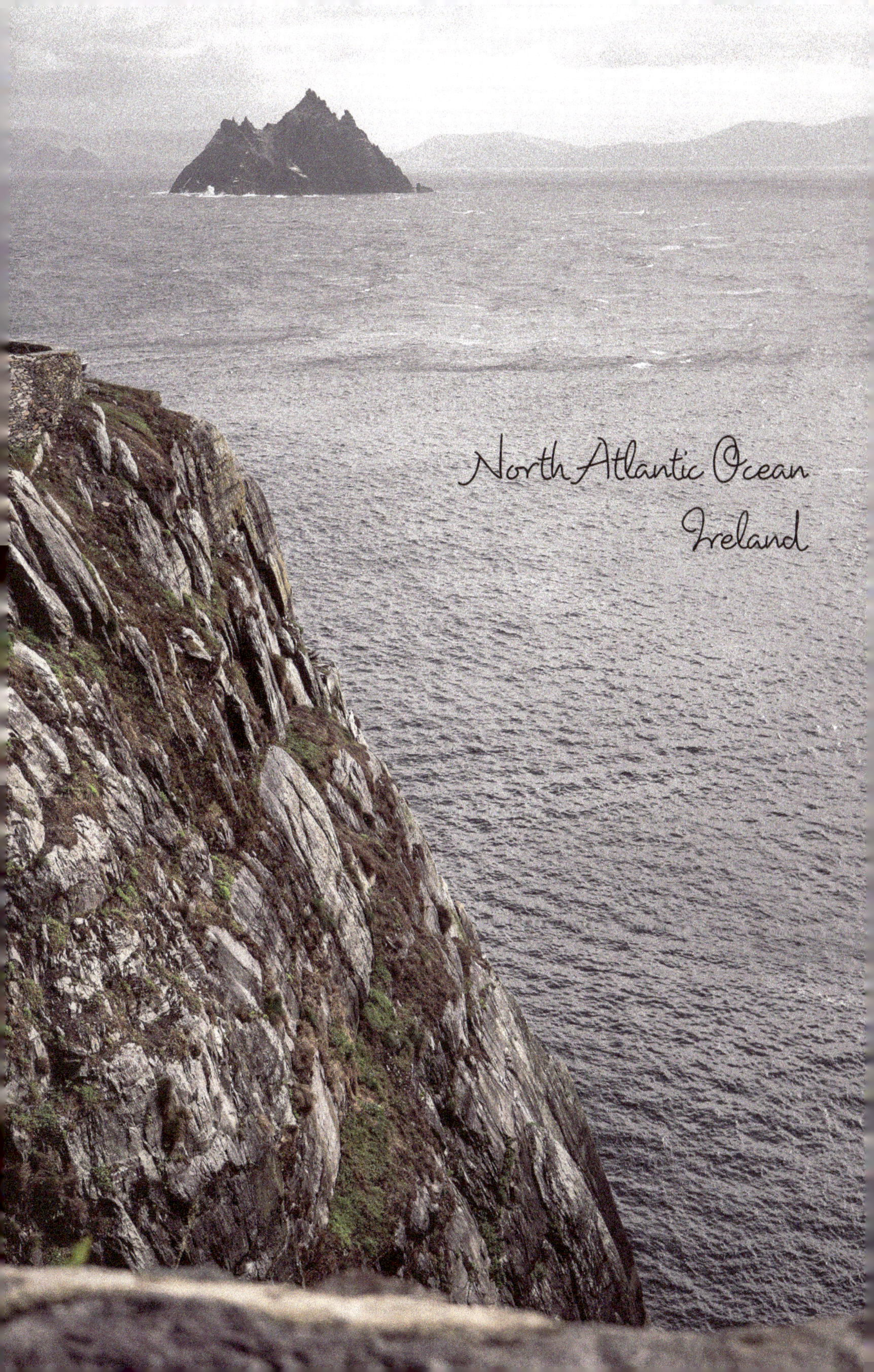
North Atlantic Ocean
Ireland

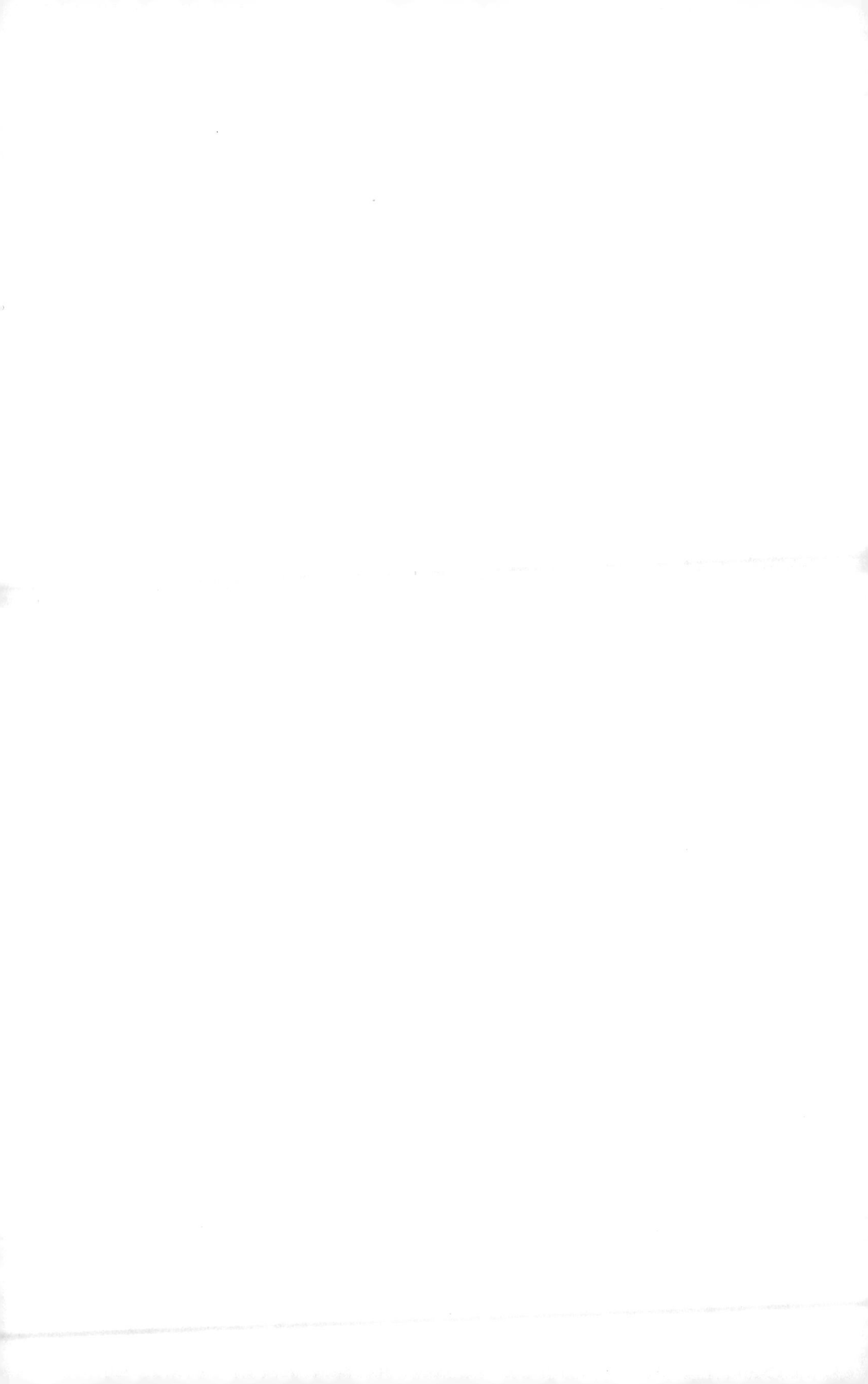

WHERE TO NEXT?

Oh, where to begin? Ever since I was a small child, I wanted to see the world. That never changed even with becoming an adult, getting a job, moving across the country, getting married, etc. The first many years of my adulthood was spent on saving money and leaping into the workforce – first in web development and then in marketing. When I met my now husband, one of the first things I told him was that I wanted to adventure far and wide. Luckily, he was right there with me (although he wasn't quite prepared for how much I would jump into any new idea I read... like the desire to sleep in a one person tent on a mountain in Oregon for a night on our honeymoon). We worked hard with the goal to eventually travel, there in the back of our minds, eventually starting with traveling around the USA. Road trips with our families and on our own. A few trips that required getting on a plane... where we found that I had a fear of taking off (go figure... at least now it has gone mostly away). And in 2015, we made the life goal to visit 100 countries and all 50 states together. We still have quite a ways to go and it will take a while to achieve as we squeeze travel in with our busy work lives and family lives. But hey... the adventure happens on the way to the goal.

I love every one of our crazy trips that we've taken so far, even the ones that go beyond my comfort zone, and I'm so honored to have been able to experience new worlds and shared moments with the people who live there. I cannot wait for more.

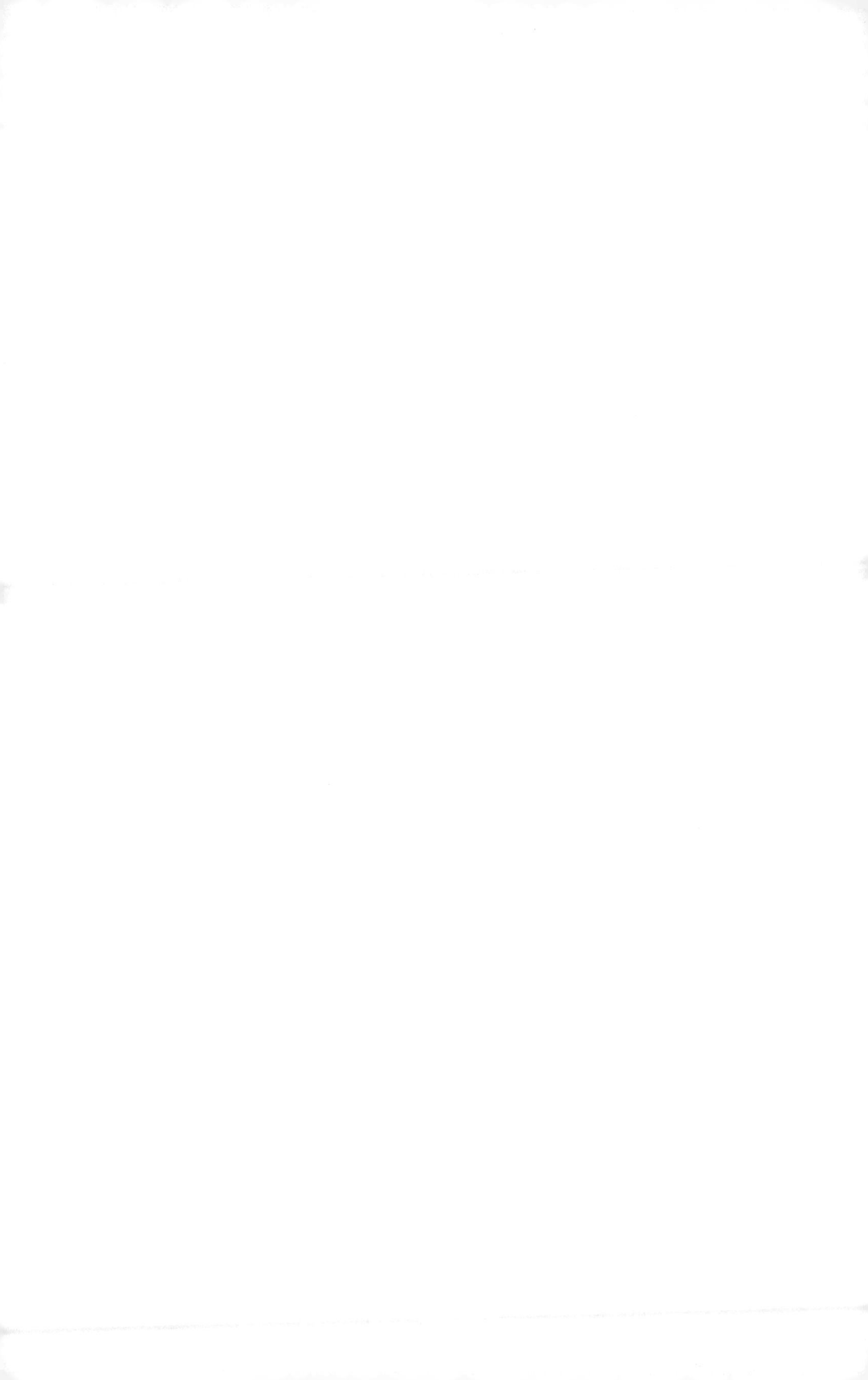

www.ingramcontent.com/pod-product-compliance
Lightning Source LLC
LaVergne TN
LVHW052346100826
845147LV00012B/766

* 9 7 8 1 7 3 5 5 1 4 0 2 4 *